1,000 Questions on ISLAM

By
Dr. Mohamed Ibrahim Elmasry

A Forward by
Dr. Jamal Badawi

Islamic Book Service

© *All Rights Reserved*

1,000 Questions on ISLAM

ISBN: 81-7231-459-0

Edition: 2003

Published by *Abdul Naeem* for
Islamic Book Service
2241, Kucha Chelan, Darya Ganj, New Delhi-110 002
Ph.: 23253514, 23265380, 23286551, Fax: 23277913
E-mail: ibsdelhi@del2.vsnl.net.in
  ibsdelhi@mantraonline.com
  islamic@eth.net
Website: http//www.islamic-india.com

Our Associates
Islamic Book Service Inc.
136, Charlotte Ave., Hicksville, N.Y. 11801.
Ph.: 516-870-0427, Fax: 516-870-0429,
Toll Free # 866-242-4IBS
E-mail: sales@islamicbookservices.com
  ibsny@conversent.net

Al Munna Book Shop Ltd.
P.O. Box-3449, **Sharjah** (U.A.E.), Tel.: 06-561-5483, 06-561-4650
E-mail: nusrat@emirates.net.ae
Dubai Branch: Tel.: 04-352-9294

Printed at: *Noida Printing Press*, C-31, Sector-7, Noida (Ghaziabad) U.P.

FORWARD TO THE SECOND EDITION

الحمد لله و الصلاة والسلام على محمد رسول الله و على آله و صحبه ومن اتبع هداه الى يوم الدين

All Praise is due to Allâh and may His peace and blessings be with Muhammad (ﷺ) the Messenger of Allâh and upon his family, his Companions and upon all who follow his guidance until the Day of Reckoning.

I had the pleasure to read Dr. Elmasry's book "One Thousand Questions on Islam". The book addresses in a simple and concise way multitudes of questions about Islam as faith and way of living. The book is solidly based on the Qur'ân, Sunnah and the position of learned scholars.

I believe that this book is of considerable benefit for more than one segment of readership. It is useful for children in giving Islamic education, a crucial need felt everywhere. In fact it is an effective tool in promoting competition among children. For a non-Muslim reader who is interested in a quick panoramic view of Islam, the book serves as a useful introduction.

I pray that Allâh (Subhana-wa-Tâ'ala) may reward my brother and friend, Dr. Mohamed Ibrahim Elmasry for his efforts and contribution to the promotion of better understanding of Islam.

                              Dr. Jamal Badawi
                              Professor, Saint Mary's University
                              Halifax, Nova Scotia, Canada

PREFACE

The need to introduce Islamic Knowledge in an interesting and effective way to a young English-speaking Muslim generation has motivated me to compile questions on different Islamic topics. These topics are included in the eight chapters of this book; Qur'ân, Hadith, Seera, Iman, Ibadat, Stories of the Prophets in the Qur'ân, Islamic History and finally Islamic Legal Rulings.

During this project I had to consult many key reference books, both in English and in Arabic. To their authors I am very grateful. Only the English references are listed. I had to choose brief, concise answers to many questions and as a result, the book relies on teachers and parents to expand on many of the answers. The references can be used for further readings and A Read-A-Thon can be arranged to encourage children to probe further using these references.

It is hoped that the book is also useful to non-Muslims who seek information regarding Islam. In a multi-faith and multi-cultural world, it is important for the young non-Muslims in the English-speaking world in general, and in the West in particular, to know the facts about the different faiths, including Islam, from reliable sources, far away from stereotypes, biased opinions and the headlines involving the actions of some Muslims.

My special thanks to Sheikh Abdul Warith Saed of Kuwait University who reviewed the Arabic version of this book.

A special note to the reader; this is the first edition of this book. I intend, God willing, to issue other revised editions with more questions. To this end, I ask you to send me your comments regarding this edition and any questions you propose to add to the next edition.

Finally, I pray to God to bless the reader, the writer and to guide us all for the best of this world and for the best in the Hereafter. Ameen.

Mohamed Ibrahim Elmasry
Waterloo, Ontario, Canada

ACKNOWLEDGEMENTS

Thanks are due to many friends who reviewed this book in part or in total: Baher Haroun, Atia El-Shakweer, Mohamed Masoud and Shoukry Lawendy. Special thanks to Sheikh Abdul Walith Saed and Sheikh Abdul Hamied-Gabier who reviewed this book, suggested many improvements and who provided support and encouragement, most needed in such a project. Thanks to my wife and to my daughter Carmen who worked on many of the early manuscripts of this book. Miss Lorna Spencer has entered and computer-edited the final manuscript of this book and to her I would like to express my appreciation.

NOTES TO THE READER

1. To the non-Muslim reader: The word Allâh in the Arabic language means God or more accurately The One and Only Eternal God, Creator of the Universe, Lord of all lords, King of all kings, Most Compassionate, Most Merciful. The word is also used by Arabic-speaking Jews and Christians. If the word Allâh does not trigger the above meaning in the mind of the non-Muslim reader, he/she can substitute the word Allâh with the word God in this book until the above meaning becomes clear.

2. To keep with Islamic traditions, when the word Allâh is mentioned in this book, the reader should add "Subhanahu-Wa-Ta'ala"; Praise all to Him the Almighty.

3. To keep with Islamic traditions we have used (ﷺ) after the word prophet which mean "Sallallâhu 'Alaihi-Wasallam"; May peace be upon him.'

4. The transliteration of the Arabic words and names in this book follows closely that used by A. Yusuf Ali in his translation of the Qur'ân.

5. In the Qur'ân, a Sûrah is a "Chapter" and it is referred to by its number. An Âyah of a Sûrah is a "verse within a chapter" and also is referred to by a number. To refer to an Âyah within a Surah the number of the Sûrah is given first and then the number of the Âyah within that Sûrah.

6. In Chapter 5, the main references was A. Sabiq, "Fiqh-us-Sunnah-Part 1" and in Chapter 8, the main reference was Y. Al-Qaradawi, "The Lawful and the Prohibited in Islam", both Published by The American Trust Publications in 1985 and 1980 respectively.

7. For comments regarding this book, for any suggested questions for the second edition, and for printing this book for free distribution, please mail to:

> Dr. M.I. Elmasry
> c/o KW Islamic Association
> 402 Clairbrook Cres.
> Waterloo, Ontario
> Canada
> N2L 5VL

CONTENTS

	PAGES
CHAPTER-1 Al-Qur'ân	1
CHAPTER-2 Al-Hadîth	21
CHAPTER-3 Al-Seera	29
CHAPTER-4 Al-Iman	45
CHAPTER-5 Al-Ibadat	59
CHAPTER-6 The Stories Of Prophets In The Qur'ân	77
CHAPTER-7 Islamic History	91
CHAPTER-8 Legal Rulings And The Lawful And Prohibited (Al-Halal And Al-Haram)	106
References	118

CHAPTER

AL-QUR'ÂN

Q. 1 What is the Qur'ân?

Ans. The Qur'ân is the word of Allâh, revealed to the last Prophet Muhammad (ﷺ) through the Angel Jibra'îl (Gabriel) (A.S.) and protected by Allâh from corruption or loss.

Q. 2 How did the Qur'ân reach us today?

Ans. By numerous persons both verbally and in writing, in the precise words as they were revealed to the Prophet (ﷺ). This process is called "tawatur".

Q. 3 What does the word Qur'ân mean?

Ans. The word is derived from the root "to read" or "to recite", hence Qur'ân is a verbal noun meaning reading or reciting.

Q. 4 What are some of the names which are used in the Qur'ân, to refer to the revelation receiving by the Prophet (ﷺ)?

Ans. Qur'ân (recitation), Furqan (criterion), Tanzil (sent down), Zikr (reminder) and Kitab (scripture).

Q. 5 What are some of the adjectives which are used in the Qur'ân to refer to the revelation received by the Prophet (ﷺ)?

Ans. Nûr (light), Rahmân (mercy), Majîd (glorious), Mubârak (blessing), Bashîr (contains glad tidings) and Nazîr (warner).

Q. 6 What does the word "Wahi" mean?

Ans. Revelation from Allâh

Q. 7 What are the purposes of revelations?

Ans. Prophets received the words of Allâh through revelations and then communicated it to their fellow human beings.

Q.8 How are revelations communicated to the Prophets?

Ans. In different ways: inspiration, like in a dream, as Allâh guided Prophet Ibrahim (A.S.) to make a sacrifice of his son; speech hidden away, as Allâh spoke to Prophet Mûsâ (A.S.) and through the Angel Jibra'îl (A.S.), as Allâh revealed the Qur'ân to Prophet Muhammad (ﷺ).

Q. 9 When did the revelation of the Qur'ân begin?

Ans. On Layla-tul-Qadr (on the 27th of Ramadan or on one of the odd nights after the 21st of Ramadan) after Prophet Muhammad (ﷺ) had reached the 40th year of his life (around the year 610 A.D.).

Q.10 Where did the Prophet (ﷺ) receive the first revelation?

Ans. In the cave of Hira on mountain near Mecca, while in seclusion.

Q.11 What were the verses of the first revelation?

Ans. The first five verses from Sûrah Al-Alaq (Sûrah no. 93): "Read, in the name of your Lord, Who created; created man form a clot of blood. Read! And your Lord is most bountiful, Who taught (the use of) the pen; He taught man which he knew not."

Q.12 Did revelations continue immediately after the first one?

Ans. No, Revelations ceased for a certain period.

Q.13 What was the second revelation?

Ans. The first beginning verses of Sûrah Al-Muddather (Sûrah no. 74) which begins as follows: "O you, who are covered in your cloak, arise and warn thy Lord magnify......."

Q.14 What were some of the early Sûrahs were revealed to the Prophet (ﷺ)?

Ans. Sûrah number 73 (Al-Muzzammil), 1 (Al-Fatiha), 81 (Al-Takweer), 87 (Al-Alla), 92 (Al-Lael) and 89 (Al-Fajr).

Q.15 For how long did the revelation continue?

Ans. For approximately 23 years, until the Prophet's (ﷺ) death, in the 10th year after Hijra (632 A.D.).

Q.16 What was one of the last revelations?

Ans. Sûrah 5: verse 4; "This day I (Allâh) have perfected your

religion for you, completed My favour upon you and have chosen for you Islam as your religion."

Q.17 Why was the Qur'ân sent down in stages?

Ans. 1. To strengthen the heart of the Prophet (ﷺ) by addressing him continuously whenever the need for guidance arose.
2. To gradually implement the laws of Allâh.
3. To make it easier for the Prophet (ﷺ) to receive the revelations, since receiving the revelations was a very exhausting experience for him.
4. To make understanding, applying and memorizing of the verses easier for the believers.

Q.18 Who was the first to commit the revelations to memory?

Ans. Prophet Muhammad (ﷺ) himself.

Q.19 Mention some well-known persons who memorized the revelations.

Ans. Some men were Abu Bakr (R.Z.A.), 'Umar (R.Z.A.), 'Ali Ibn Mas'ûd (R.Z.A.), Abu Hurairah (R.Z.A.), 'Abdullâh Ibn 'Abbâs (R.Z.A.) and 'Abdullah Ibn 'Amr Ibn 'Al'as (R.Z.A.). Some women were 'Aisha (R.Z.A.), Hafsa (R.Z.A.), and Umm Salma (R.Z.A.).

Q.20 Who were the companions who had memorized the Qur'ân in its entirety and gone over it with the Prophet (ﷺ) before his death?

Ans. Ubai Ibn Ka'ab (R.Z.A.), Mu'âz Ibn Jabal (R.Z.A.) and Zaid Ibn Thâbit (R.Z.A.).

Q.21 Was the Qur'ân written down during the lifetime of the Prophet (ﷺ)?

Ans. Yes, but it was not bound as a single volume.

Q.22 Did the Prophet (ﷺ) write down the revelations?

Ans. No, he dictated the revelations to some forty-eight companions among them Zaid Ibn Thâbit (R.Z.A.).

Q.23 Were there any reports that the Qur'ân was written down during the lifetime of the Prophet (ﷺ)?

Ans. Yes, among these reports is the fact that when people came to

Madinah to learn about Islam, they were provided with copies of the chapters of the Qur'ân, to read and memorize.

Q.24. Did the Prophet (ﷺ) give instructions for the arrangement of the verses of the Qur'ân?

Ans. Yes, the order and the arrangement was well known to the Muslims due to the daily recitation of the Qur'ân in their prayers.

Q.25 Who used to recite the Qur'ân once a year with the Prophet (ﷺ)?

Ans. Angel Jibra'îl (A.S.) and he recited it twice with him the year he died.

Q.26 What was the shape of the Qur'ân when the Prophet (ﷺ) died?

Ans. All the parts of the Qur'ân and its order and arrangement were available both in written form, in separate written material (Suhuf) and memorized by the companions.

Q.27 What is the difference between Suhuf and Mushaf?

Ans. Suhuf (plural, singular; Sahifah) means loose pieces of writing material such as paper, dry animal skin, papyrus...etc., while Mushaf (singular, plural; Masahif) means collected Suhuf brought together into fixed order, between two covers into a bound volume.

Q.28 What form was the Qur'ân in during the Prophet's (ﷺ) time and during Abu Bakr's (R.Z.A.) and 'Umar's (R.Z.A.) time?

Ans. It was in the form of Suhuf, the order of the verses within each Sûrah was fixed, but the sheets on which the Sûrah was written were still in a loose arrangement. i.e. not bound into a volume.

Q.29 Who ordered the Qur'ân to be bounded into a volume; Mushaf?

Ans. 'Uthman (R.Z.A.).

Q.30 What led Uthman (R.Z.A.) to order the collection of the Qur'ân into a Mushaf?

Ans. 1. During Abu Bakr's (R.Z.A.) rule, he instructed Zaid Ibn

Thabit (R.Z.A.) to collect the Qur'ân from the various written material and from the memories of people. The collection was kept with him and then with Umar (R.Z.A.) and then with his daughter Hafsa (R.Z.A.).

2. During Uthman's (R.Z.A.) rule, disputes had arisen among Muslims in the vast Muslim empire about the correct manner of reciting the Qur'ân.

3. Uthman (R.Z.A.) borrowed the suhuf, which were kept with Hafsa (R.Z.A.) and ordered four companions among them Zaid Ibn Thabit (R.Z.A.) to rewrite the script in perfect copies.

4. Uthman (R.Z.A.) sent these copies to the main centres of the Muslim world to replace other copies that were in circulation. This copy of the Qur'ân has remained the same to this day.

Q.31 What are the differences between the printed form of today's Mushaf and that of Uthman's (R.Z.A.)?

Ans. Today's Mushaf has vowelling marks (tashkil) to help in the pronunciation and diacritical marks to help tell the difference between similar letters. All old Qur'ânic script is completely without diacritical points or vowels signs. Also there are no headings or separations between the Swar or any other kind of division or formal indication of the end of a verse.

Q.32 Do we still have old manuscripts of the Qur'ân?

Ans. Yes. In the Egyptian National Library there is a copy made on gazelle skin which has been dated 68 after Hijra (688 A.D.), 58 years after the Prophet's (ﷺ) death. There are also copies from the first and second centuries A.H.

Q.33 When were diacritical marks and vowelling symbols introduced into the Qur'ânic manuscript?

Ans. First century A.H.

Q.34 When was the first time the current manuscript of the Qur'ân printed?

Ans. In 1925 (1344 A.H.) in Cairo, Egypt and it is based on the reading of Hafs as reported by Asim.

Q.35 What is an "Âyah" (pl. Âyat)?

Ans. Âyah means a sign and in the Qur'ân it refers to a Qur'ânic verse.

Q.36 What is a "Sûrah" (pl. Swar)?

Ans. Sûrah is derived from the Arabic word "Soor", meaning fence and in the Qur'ân it refers to a Qur'ânic Chapter.

Q.37 How many Sûrah are there in the Qur'ân?

Ans. 114 (one hundred and fourteen).

Q.38 Do all the Sûrah of the Qur'ân have the same number of Âyah?

Ans. No.

Q.39 How many Âyah is there in the longest Sûrah?

Ans. 286 (two hundred and eighty-six).

Q.40 Which is the longest Sûrah?

Ans. Al-Baqara (No. 2).

Q.41 How many Âyah is there in the shortest Sûrah?

Ans. 3 (three)

Q.42 Name one of the shortest Sûrah?

Ans. Al-'Asr (No. 103).

Q.43 Do all Sûrah begin with (*Bismillâhir-Rahmânir-Rahîm*)?

Ans. No; all except Sûrah no. 9.

Q.44 Do all Sûrah have titles (names or headings)?

Ans. Yes.

Q.45 Who determined the arrangement of the Swar?

Ans. The Prophet (ﷺ) under guidance from Angel Jibra'îl (A.S.).

Q.46 How did scholars group the Swar into four groups?

Ans. 1. The long ones (Al-Tiwal); No. 2 to 10.
2. The medium length ones (Al-ma'ûn); each approximately 100 Âyat in length; No. 11 to 35.
3. Al-Methana; each less than 100 Âyat in length; No. 36 to 49.
4. Al-Mufassal; the last section; No. 50 to 114.

Q.47 What is Juz' (pl. Ajza')?

Ans. Juz' means part of portion and in the Qur'ân it refers to be 30 juz' of approximately equal length into which the Qur'ân is divided.

Q.48 What is Hizb (pl. Ahzab)?

Ans. Each Juz' in the Qur'ân is subdivided into four Hizb, where each Hizb is subdivided into quarters; first quarter of the Hizb, half and third quarter.

Q.49 Can you call the translation of the Qur'ân the Qur'ân?

Ans. No, it is an interpretation of the original Arabic text in a given language.

Q.50 Is understanding Arabic a prerequisite to fully grasp the meaning of the Qur'ân?

Ans. Yes.

Q.51 Can you make use of translations to indirectly know the meaning of the Qur'ân?

Ans. Yes.

Q.52 Is it easy to understand the Qur'ân?

Ans. Yes, when you try. "We have indeed made the Qur'ân easy to be remembered (and to be understood). Is there anyone that remembers (and understands) it." 54:17

Q.53 Is the text of the Qur'ân in Arabic prose or poetry?

Ans. Neither, it is a unique style of unmatched beauty and quality. It is Allâh's last words to guide mankind.

Q.54 Does the Qur'ân contain stories (Qasas, sg. Qissah)?

Ans. Yes. "We do relate unto thee the most beautiful of stories." 12:3

Q.55 What are the Qur'ânic stories about?

Ans. 1. Prophets of Allâh, their people, their messages, their calls …etc., for example Nûh (A.S.) (Noah), Mûsâ (A.S.) (Moses), and 'Îsa (A.S.) (Jesus).

2. Past people or events, eg. the Companions of the cave.

3. Events that took place during the lifetime of the Prophet (), eg. battle of Badr.

Q.56 Does the Qur'ân use examples, similes (am<u>th</u>al, sg. ma<u>th</u>al) to explain a message?

Ans. Yes.

Q.57 What is the meaning of 'Qul'?

Ans. Say, which is an instruction to the Prophet () to address the words, following this word, to his audience.

Q.58 How many times is the word 'Qul' used in the Qur'ân?
Ans. More than 200 (two hundred) times.

Q.59 Does the Qur'ân use oath-like expressions (aqsam, sg. qasam)?
Ans. Yes.

Q.60 How does the oath-like expressions start?
Ans. 'Wa' meaning 'and', or 'la-uqsimu' meaning 'indeed I swear' or using the letter 'ta'.

Q.61 Why is the oath-like expression used in the Qur'ân?
Ans. To strengthen and support an argument, to get the attention of the reader and to point out the magnificent event or phenomenon.

Q.62 What is the meaning of 'Mohkamat' as it refers to certain Âyat of the Qur'ân?
Ans. 'Mohkamat' is derived from the Arabic root "hakama" meaning to decide and it is used to refer to Âyat of the Qur'ân which have only one interpretation.

Q.63 What is the meaning of 'mutashabihat, sg. mutashabiha' as it refers to certain Âyat of the Qur'ân?
Ans. It is derived from the Arabic root 'shubbiha' meaning look-alike and it is used to refer to Âyat of the Qur'ân which have more than one interpretation.

Q.64 What is the topic of Âyat belonging to the 'Mohkamat'?
Ans. Âyat dealing with legal ruling (halal and haram), punishment, inheritance, promises and threats .... etc.

Q.65 What is the topic of Âyat belonging to the 'Mutashabihat'?
Ans. Âyat dealing with attributes of Allâh, the true nature of the resurrection and judgement and life after death .... etc.

Q.66 What is the name of the Âyat applicable in general?
Ans. "Al-'am" which is applicable in general, eg. to all human beings, or to all Muslims...etc.

Q.67 What is the name of the Âyat applicable to certain special circumstances?
Ans. "Al-Khas" which is applicable with some kind of condition or specified limitation.

Q.68 What are the two types of Âyat which deals with legal rulings (ahkam)?

Ans. There are the Âyat which are free from any conditions (Mutlaq) and there are the Ayât which are bound by special conditions (Muqayyad).

Q.69 What is the Arabic word used to refer to those Âyat whose meaning are derived from the literal wording?

Ans. 'Mantuq'.

Q.70 What is the Arabic word used to refer to those Âyat whose meaning are derived from the context?

Ans. 'Mufhum'.

Q.71 What is the Arabic word used to refer to those separate letters with which some Sûrah begin?

Yes. 'Al-Muqatta-ât'.

Q.72 How many Sûrah starts with separate letter Âyah?

Ans. 29 (twenty-nine).

Q.73 How many letters are used in forming the separate letter Ayât?

Yes. 14 (fourteen).

Q.74 List the letters with which some Sûrah starts and their Sûrah number.

Ans. Alif Lâm Râ: 10, 11, 12, 14 and 15.

Alif Lâm Mîm: 2, 3, 29, 30, 31 and 32.

Alif Lâm Mîm Râ: 13.

Alif Lâm Sâd: 7

Ha Mîm: 40, 41, 42, 43, 44, 45 and 46.

Sâd: 38

Ta Sîn: 27.

Tâ Hâ: 20.

Qâf: 50.

Kâf Hâ Yâ A'in Sâd: 19

Nûn: 68

Yâ Sîn: 36

Tâ Sîn Mîm: 26, 28.

Q.75 **What is the significance of using separate letters at the beginning of some Sûrah?**

Ans. The exact significance is known to Allâh, but Muslim scholars have many explanations. A widely used one is that they are used to draw the attention of the listener to the fact that the following are Allâh's words. Although they consist of the Arabic alphabet, they have a unique beauty and style and offer a guidance to mankind.

Q.76 **When is a Sûrah called a "Makkiya"; Meccan Sûrah?**

Ans. When its beginning was revealed before Hijra.

Q.77 **When is a Sûrah called a "Madaniya"; Medinian Sûrah?**

Ans. When its beginning was revealed after Hijra, even if some ayat are revealed before Hijra.

Q.78 **What are the main topics of the Meccan Sûrah?**

Ans. 1. Allâh and His unity (Tawheed).
2. Resurrection and Judgement.
3. Righteous conduct.

Q.79 **What were the main topics of the Medinian Sûrah?**

Ans. In addition to the same topics of the 'Meccan Sûrah', new topics were added. eg. legal rulings, addressing the people of the book (Jews and Christians).

Q.80 **How many Sûrah are of Meccan origin?**

Ans. 85 (eighty-five).

Q.81 **How many Sûrah are of the Medinian origin?**

Ans. 29 (twenty-nine).

Q.82 **How many juz' (part) does the Mekkan Sûrah constitute?**

Ans. 11 (eleven).

Q.83 **How many juz' (part) does the Medinian Sûrah constitute?**

Ans. 19 (nineteen). Note that although the Mediniyan Sûrah are fewer in number they are longer.

Q.84 **What is the length of the Meccan ayat relative to the Mediniyan ayat?**

Ans. The Meccan Âyat are often shorter than the Medinian ayat.

Q.85 What are the first 5 (five) Sûrah which were revealed?

Ans. Sûrah 96, 68, 73, 74 and 111.

Q.86 Why is it important to know the chronology of the Swar and ayat, although the Qur'ân is not arranged in chronological order?

Ans. To understand the gradual guidance given by Allâh to form a nation (Ummah) of believers.

Q.87 What is the meaning of 'Asbab-Al-Nuzûl'?

Ans. The particular circumstances, events and reasons of a certain revelation.

Q.88 What is the meaning of 'Tafsîr'?

Ans. The explanation and interpretation of the Qur'ân.

Q.89 Why is knowing 'Asbab-Al-Nuzûl' important in 'Tafsîr'?

Ans. It is important because it helps in understanding the direct and immediate meaning and implication of an Âyah.

Q.90 Who related to us "Asbab-Al-Nuzûl"?

Ans. The Companions of the Prophet (ﷺ).

Q.91 What is the meaning of 'Shari'ah?

Ans. Legal ruling given by Allâh in the Qur'ân or the Sunnah of His Prophet.

Q.92 Did other Prophets before Muhammed (ﷺ) bring particular 'Shari'ah' to their people?

Ans. Yes.

Q.93 Are there any differences between the last shari'ah and the others?

Ans. Yes.

Q.94 Are there any differences between the call for basic beliefs between the last call and the other calls before the Prophet Muhammad (ﷺ)?

Ans. No. The call was the same, to worship and to submit to one God; it is the call of Islam.

Q.95 During the call to Islâm by the Prophet (ﷺ), were the legal rulings (ahkam) updated by Allâh?

Ans. Yes.

Q.96 What are the ten readings of the Qur'ân?

Ans. They refer to the changes in pronouncing some Âyat and the way they sound.

Q.97 What is the most common method of reciting the Qur'ân?

Ans. The recitation transmitted to us by Hafs (180 A.H.) from 'Âsim (127 A.H.)

Q.98 What is the method of reciting the Qur'ân which is widely used in North Africa (except Egypt)?

Ans. The recitation transmitted to us by Warsh (197 A.H.) from Nafi' (169 A.H.).

Q.99 What conditions must a given method of reciting the Qur'ân fulfill?

Ans. The recitation must agree with Arabic grammar, agree with the written text of 'Uthmân' (R.Z.A.), and traced back reliably to the Prophet (ﷺ) by many companions (Mutawatir).

Q.100 What are the meanings of 'tafsîr' and 'ta'wîl?

Ans. Tafsîr is from the root 'fassara' meaning to explain, to expound and refers to the explanation, interpretation and commentary on the Qur'ân. Ta'wîl is from the root 'awala' meaning also to explain and refers to, as the word 'tafsîr', the interpretation of the Qur'ân.

Q.101 What is the meaning of 'mufassir', pl. 'mufassirîn'?

Ans. It refers to the Muslim scholar who does the 'tafsîr', ie. commentator.

Q.102 What are the qualifications a 'mufassir' must have?

Ans. 1. Be of sound and strong belief (aqîda).

2. Be fluent in the Arabic language, mastering its grammar, structures, etc.

3. Be highly qualified in Islâmic sciences, eg. Hadîth.

4. Refers to other 'tafsîr' and to reports of the Prophet (ﷺ), his companions (Sahaba) and their followers (tabi'în).

5. Abstains from using unfounded explanation.

Q.103 What are the basic rules of doing a 'tafsîr'?

Ans. To explain the Qur'ân by using other parts of the Qur'ân, by using the Prophet's (ﷺ) Sunnah, by using reports from the sahaba and finally the reports from tabi'ûn.

Q.104 What are the types of 'tafsîr'?

1. Bil-riwaya; by transmission, by using the Qur'ân, Sunnah and reports of the sahaba and tabi'ûn.

2. Bil-ray; by sound opinion which include the above sources as in (1) in addition to using reason and scholarly studies (ijtihâd).

3. Bil-ishara, by indication from guided signs given by Allâh and not entirely based on the science of 'tafsir' at a given time.

The last type of 'tafsir' is not accepted.

Q.105 Who are the most famous Sahaba, whose reports are useful in 'tafsîr'?

Ans. Abu Bakr (R.Z.A.), Umar (R.Z.A.), Uthman (R.Z.A.), Ali, Ibn Mas'ûd (R.Z.A.), Ibn Abbas (R.Z.A.), Ubay Ibn Ka'b (R.Z.A.), Zaid Ibn Thabit (R.Z.A.), Abu Mûsâ Al-Ashari (R.Z.A.) and Abdullâh Ibn Zubair (R.Z.A.).

Q.106 Who is the most famous 'mufassirîn' from the 'tabi'în' who were living in Mekka and who were taught by 'Abdullâh Ibn 'Abbâs?

Ans. Mujâhid (d.104 A.H.).

Q.107 Who are the most famous 'mufassirîn' from the 'tabi'în' who were living in Medina and who were taught by Ubay Ibn Ka'b (R.Z.A.)?

Ans. Muhammad Ibn Ka'b al-Qurzi (R.Z.A.) (d.117 A.H.). Abu-l 'Alliya al-Riyahi (R.Z.A.) (d.90 A.H.) and Zaid Ibn Aslam (R.Z.A.) (d.130 A.H.)

Q.108 Who are the most famous 'mufassireen' from the tabi'een' who were living in Iraq and who were taught by Ibn Mas'ûd (R.Z.A.)?

Ans. Al-Hassan al-Basri (d.121 A.H.), Masrook Ibn al-'Ajda (d.63 A.H.) and Ibrahim al-Nakhai' (d.95 A.H.).

Q.109 List the most important 'tafsîr'?

Ans.
1. Tafsîr al-Tabari (d.310 A.H.)
2. Tafsîr Ibn-Kathîr (d.774 A.H.)
3. Tafsîr al-Suyuti (d.911 A.H.)
4. Tafsîr al-Zamakhshari (d.539 A.H.)
5. Tafsîr al-Razi (d.606 A.H.)
6. Tafsîr al-Baidawi (d.685 A.H.)
7. Tafsîr al-Jalalain (d.911 A.H.)
8. Tafsîr al-Manar (d.1354 A.H.)
9. Fizilal-al-Qur'ân (d.1386 A.H.)
10. Tafhîm-al-Qur'ân (d.1400 A.H.).

and among others are Tafsîr Al-Qurtobee and Tafsîr Al-Nasfee.

Q.110 Who wrote Tafsir al-Tabari?

Ans. Ibn Jarir al-Tabari who lived in Iraq and travelled to Egypt and Syria.

Q.111 What is the title of Tafsîr al-Tabari?

Ans. Jami al-Bayan the tafsîr al-Qur'ân.

Q.112 What characterizes Tafsîr al-Tabari?

Ans. It belongs to the class of tafsîr bil-riwaya and is based on reports from the Prophet (), the Sahaba and the Tabi'een.

Q.113 How important is Tafsîr al-Tabari?

Ans. One of the voluminous scholarly works (30 volumes) and one of the early tafsîr which is referred to by almost every subsequent scholar. It was printed in Egypt in 1903, 1911 and 1954. No English translation is available.

Q.114 Who wrote Tafsîr Ibn Kathîr?

Ans. Ismail Ibn Amr Ibn Kathîr who lived in Damascus and was the student of Ibn Tymia.

Q.115 What is the title of Tafsîr Ibn Kathir?
Ans. Tafsîr Al-Qur'ân Al-zaim.

Q.116 How important is Tafsîr Ibn Kathîr?
Ans. One of the widely used, with emphasis on soundness of reports, referring a reader to other relevant ayat on the topic discussed. No English translation is available.

Q.117 Who wrote Tafsîr al-Suyuti?
Ans. Jalal al-Deen al-Suyuti.

Q.118 What is the title of Tafsîr al-Suyuti?
Ans. Al-Duir al-manthur fee al-tafsîr al-ma'thur.

Q.119 Who wrote Tafsîr al-Razi?
Ans. Mohammed Ibn Umar al-Razi.

Q.120 What is the title of Tafsîr al-Razi?
Ans. Mafateeh al-Ghaib.

Q.121 What characterizes Tafsîr al - Razi?
Ans. One of the most comprehensive work of the type of tafsîr bil-ray' covering many areas in length; eg. one volume in tafsîr al-Fatiha. It is also known as al-Tafsîr al-Kabeer (the large Tafsîr).

Q.122 Who wrote Tafsîr al-manar?
Ans. Muhammad Rashid Rida the well known student of Imam Muhammed Abduh (d 1323) of Egypt.

Q.123 What characterizes Tafsîr al-manar?
Ans. The Tafsîr is in 12 volumes covering only about (1/3) of the Qur'ân, since its author died before completing it. The Tafsîr refers to current everyday problems facing Muslims.

Q.124 Who wrote Fizilal-al Qur'ân (in the Shade of the Qur'ân)?
Ans. Sayid Qutb of Egypt, mostly during his imprisonment (1954 - 1964) and completed before he was executed by the Egyptian government because of his association with the Islamic movement, Ikhwan al-Muslimeen.

Q.125 What characterizes Fizilal-al Qur'ân?
Ans. The author emphasized the difference between Islam and the

non-Islamic systems, as well as the need to establish Islam on the individual and the social level. The last part has been translated into English.

Q.126 Who wrote Tafhîm-al-Qur'ân (Understanding the Qur'ân)?

Ans. Abul 'Ala Mawdudi of India.

Q.127 What characterizes Tafhîm-al-Qur'ân?

Ans. Written in Urdu, completed in 1973 and has been translated into English. One of the best available complete tafsir in English.

Q.128 Why is it difficult to translate the Qur'ân?

Ans. Because words in different languages do not express all the shades of meanings of their counterparts and the translation would never adequately express the beauty of the original text.

Q.129 Were parts of the Qur'ân translated to other languages in the time of the Prophet (ﷺ)?

Ans. Yes, when the Prophet (ﷺ) sent a message to Herachius, the Byzantine emperor it contained an Âyah (3:64), the message was translated including that Âyah. Also, the Muslims translated ayat from Sûrah Maryam (19) regarding the Prophet 'Îsa (A.S.) (Christ) in front of the emperor of Abyssinia (Ethiopia today).

Q.130 What is the most important English translation of the Qur'ân?

Ans. 1. M. Pickthall
2. 'Abdullâh Yusuf 'Ali

Q.131 What are the conditions which must be fulfilled by a translator so that the translation would be accepted by Muslims?

Ans. He/she must be a Muslim with a strong sound belief; knowledgeable with Arabic, especially the language of the Qur'ân and the language to be used for the translation and other related Islamic Sciences, e.g. Hadîth, Tafsîr, ...etc.

Q.132 What is the definition of a miracle (mo'jeza) from Allâh?

Ans. An event which happens through a messenger only by the

will of Allâh, the Creator. It breaks the usual norms and serves as a proof for the truth and the claim by the messenger that he is the messenger of Allâh.

Q.133 Why is the Qur'ân called a miracle?

1. Its language and style excels all other texts of the Arabic language.
2. Its comprehensiveness cannot be matched.
3. Its legislation and legal rulings and their sophistication cannot be surpassed.
4. Its narrations about the unknown can only result from a revelation from the creator (eg. creation of the Universe, Day of Judgement, Paradise, Hell fire, Stories of Prophets, etc.)
5. It has no contradiction with the most advanced sound discovery of all branches of science.
6. Its fulfilment of all its prophecies.
7. Its complete harmony with human natural needs (fitra).
8. It speaks to the human heart as well as the human faculty of reason at the individual level and at the group (Umma, Jamâ'ah) level.
9. It was delivered 1417 years ago by a messenger who could not read nor write.
10. It transformed a group of 100,000 early Muslims through a quantum and giant step to be the best examples for humanity in only 23 years.
11. It answers the most important questions in human life, eg. Why are we here?, Who created us?, What happens after we die?, What about the nations before us?, What is right and wrong?, How can you be happy?, etc.
12. It corrects the current belief among the people of the Book (the Christians as they say that Christ is the Son of God or He is God himself and their belief in the original sin... etc. and the Jews as they say that they are the chosen people and they have a special private covenant with God and not to preach the Book of Mûsâ (Torah) and only a Jew is appointed by God for special missions...etc.).

13. The consistence in using beautiful language throughout 23 years during its revelation in expressing wide varieties of topics from moral ethics to complex legal rulings, to belief, to stories of Prophets, to acts of worship, ...etc.

14. No other piece of literature, in any language, can match its combined beauty and sophistication, touching the heart and the mind.

15. Its teaching strikes a well measured and balanced approach to all aspects of human needs, e.g. making a living and praying.

16. The Qur'ân is a unique, supreme book of guidance from the Lord of the Universe (Rab-al-Âlamîn). If it is followed, the Lord guarantees the success in this life and in the hearafter. Throughout Islamic history, this fact has been proven time and time again; at the individual level and at the group and national levels: when the Qur'ân is followed success comes generously.

Q.134 Mention examples of how the Qur'ân contained scientific facts only discovered by modern science in the last 50 years?

Ans.
1. The earth was previously part of the Sun and only after separation, it became a habitable place for mankind (21:30).
2. All life originated from water (21:30).
3. The Universe was in the shape of a fiery gas (41:11).
4. Matter is made up of minute particles (10:62).
5. The oxygen content of the air is reduced at higher altitudes (6:125).
6. Everything consists of complementary elements (equivalent to male and female); animals, man, plants and inorganic material (36:36).
7. The embryo in the womb is enclosed by three coverings (39:6).
8. The fertilization of certain plants is done by the wind (15:22).
9. Microscopic organisms exist that are not visible to the naked eye (96:1).
10. Each human has permanent individual fingerprints (75:4).

Q.135 If the Qur'ân contains facts which agree with the discovery of sciences today, does this mean that it is a book of science?

Ans. No, it is a book of guidance for mankind from Allâh, the Creator, the Lord of the Universe. Scientific facts are not absolute truths, they change as our knowledge changes. The Qur'ân contains a guidance to the Truth.

Q.136 What are the rules which you have to observe regarding reading the Qur'ân?

Ans. 1. You should have your personal copy of the Qur'ân, kept in a clean place.

2. Read the Qur'ân regularly, daily if possible at a given time, alone or with others.

3. Concentrate, reflect, understand as you seek Allâh's guidance by reading.

4. Begin with "*a'ûzu billâhî Minash-shaytânir-Rajîm*" (I seek Allâh's refuge from Satan), "*Bismillâhir-Rahmânir-Rahîm*" (In the name of Allâh, the Most Merciful, the Most Compassionate).

5. Be ritually clean (have Wudu').

6. Read with a good voice and pronounce its words correctly.

7. Memorize as much as you can.

8. Apply it in your daily life and encourage others to read and apply it in their daily lives.

9. Say when you finish "*Saddaqa Allâhû al A'zîm*" (Allâh the All Mighty told the Truth).

10. Interrupt, when you hear Azan (call for prayer) and when somebody says "*Al-Salamu-'Alaikum*".

Q.137 What is Sajda-al-Tilawa?

Ans. It is the prostration you perform (Similar to the one you do during a Rak'a of Salah) when you read or listen to a specific ayah (fourteen places in the Qur'ân).

Q.138 What is "tajweed"?

Ans. It is derived from the Arabic root (jawwada), meaning (to make well) and refers to the rules of proper pronunciation, speed at which you read the Qur'ân and the correct length and emphasis given to vowels.

Q.139 Why is memorizing the Qur'ân so important?

Ans. The Qur'ân is the only book in human history that has been orally transmitted in its entirety through generations. Memorizing it today keeps such an outstanding achievement alive and well. Memorizing it has been ordered by the Prophet (ﷺ). Ayat from the Qur'ân are used to perform prayer (Salah) and making do'ah (private prayer).

Q.140 Mention some practical suggestions to help in memorizing the Qur'ân.

Ans.
1. Make it a daily routine.
2. Try to memorize a few ayat at a time.
3. Select ayat which are easy for you to memorize after you understand its meaning.
4. Use these ayat in your Salah.
5. Use the help of another person, tape or writing it yourself.

Q.141 Mention some of the well-known scholarly reciters of the Qur'ân where their recitations of the whole Qur'ân is preserved on tapes.

Ans. Sheikh Mahmood Khalil Al-Hussari, Abd al-Basit Abdel-Samad, Mahmood Aly Al-Bana, Mohammad Mahmood Ali Al-Tablawee, Mohammad Sadiq Al-Menshawy, Mustafa Ismail, all of Egypt and Abdullah Al-khayyat and Ali Abdel Rahman Al-Khazafee of Saudi Arabia, and the best known lady reciter is Nur Asiah Djamil of Indonesia.

CHAPTER 2

AL-HADÎTH

Q. 1 What is Hadîth?

Ans. Hadîth or tradition are records of what the Prophet (ﷺ) said, practices, and his way of life. It also included any action done in his presence by any of his disciples and if they were approved or not prohibited by him.

Q. 2 What is the meaning of the word "Hadîth"?

Ans. Statement.

Q.3 What is Sunnah?

Ans. The practices of the Prophet (ﷺ). It has the same meaning as Hadîth.

Q. 4 Should Muslims follow the Sunnah of the Prophet (ﷺ)?

Ans. Yes, as the Qur'ân confirms: "Certainly, there is for you (Muslims), in the Messenger of Allâh an excellent example." (33:21).

Q. 5 What is the difference between the Qur'ân and the sayings (Hadîth) of the Prophet (ﷺ)?

Ans. The Qur'ân contains only Allâh's words as transmitted through the angel Gabriel (A.S.) to the Prophet (ﷺ). the Hadîth was inspired by Allâh and the words were those of the Prophet (ﷺ).

Q. 6 Is every action of the Prophet (ﷺ) Hadîth?

Ans. No, the Prophet (ﷺ) had his personal opinions and advice he gave as an ordinary man does not come under Hadîth.

Q.7 Is there any difference in the language of the Qur'ân and that of the Hadîth?

Ans. Yes. The Arabic language of the Qur'ân is superb and holds out a challenge to the Arabic language scholars to produce even one of its verses. The Arabic language of the Hadîth, although excellent, does not excel to the standard of the language of the Qur'ân.

Q. 8 What is Allâh's commitment towards the Qur'ân?

Ans. That it will remain uncorrupt without change of a single word and Allâh will preserve it intact until the Day of Judgement. As He says in the Qur'ân, "We have, without doubt, sent down the message and We will, assuredly guard it (from corruption)." 15:9.

Q. 9 How are prayers (Salah) specified in the Qur'ân and the Hadîth?

Ans. The Qur'ân specifies that prayers are obligatory and should be offered at given times. The details are given in Hadîth, their number, character, how they are performed and the recitations at each stage.

Q.10 How are Zakah (paying the alms) specified in the Qur'ân and the Hadîth?

Ans. The Qur'ân specifies that Zakah is obligatory and should be given to the needy, etc. The rules and regulations for its payment and collection are given by the Prophet's (ﷺ) example.

Q.11 Can a Muslim follow only the Qur'ân but not the Hadîth?

Ans. No, as in the Qur'ân, "Say (O Muhammad (ﷺ) to the Muslims) if you love Allâh, then walk in my footsteps and Allâh will love you. "3:31 and "Those who disobey Allâh and His Prophet (ﷺ) and transgress His limits will be admitted to a fire, to abide therein and they shall have a humiliating punishment." 4:14.

Q.12 What is Ijma?

Ans. Agreement of Muslim scholars on a question of law not dealt with directly by the Qur'ân and the Hadîth. Ijma may be based on a text or an analogy mentioned in the Qur'ân or in the Hadîth.

Q.13 What is Qiyas or Rai?

Ans. Private judgement by a Muslim scholar or a group of scholars on a question of law, deducted from the Qur'ân, Hadîth and Ijma.

Q.14 How do we know that Muslim Scholars are allowed to use their judgement in a matter of law not directly given in Qur'ân and Hadîth (Sunnah)?

Ans. When the Prophet (ﷺ) posted Muaz ibn Jabal as a Governor of

Yemen, he asked him how he would decide a matter that came up to him for a decision. He replied that he would decide according to Qur'ân, if he did not find it there he would decide according to the Sunnah and if he did not find it would be according to his own opinion. The Prophet was pleased with his answers and approved of them.

Q.15 Can Ijma, Qiyas (Rai) override the specific provisions of the Qur'ân and Hadîth?

Yes. No.

Q.16 Did the Prophet (ﷺ) encourage Muslims who heard his teachings or who saw his actions to tell other Muslims who were not present?

Ans. Yes. He said his preachings should be conveyed to those who were not present and that such an act would be rewarded by Allâh. He also warned that if any one attributed any saying to him which was not uttered by him, his place would be Hell.

Q.17 Mention five people who conveyed most of the Prophet's (ﷺ) sayings and actions to other Muslims.

Ans. His wife 'Aisha (R.Z.A.) who had a remarkable memory and who lived for 48 years after his death (2210 Hadîth). His companion Abu Hurairah (R.Z.A.) (5374 Hadîth), who was constantly with the Prophet (ﷺ) and who had no worries about earning his livlihood as he was the Prophet's (ﷺ) guest. His servant Anas (R.Z.A.)(2286 Hadith), Abdullâh Ibn Umar (R.Z.A.) (2630 Hadîth), Abdullâh Ibn Abbas (R.Z.A.) (1660 Hadîth).

Q.18 What incentives did the Muslims who conveyed the Prophet's (ﷺ) saying have to convey these saying?

Ans. These Muslims were faithful followers and companions who loved the Prophet (ﷺ) very much and were ever ready to pick up and preserve any of his sayings or actions.

Q.19 Was the Prophet's (ﷺ) Hadîth conveyed in writing or by the memory of his companions?

Ans. Both.

Q.20 Were there any early ways to teach Muslims about the Prophet's (ﷺ) Hadîth after his death?

Ans. Yes, Abu Hurairah (R.Z.A.) opened a school with 800 students where he taught Hadîth. Also Caliph Umar (R.Z.A.) sent companions like Abdullâh ibn Mas'ûd (R.Z.A.) and Abu Hurairah (R.Z.A.) to the different parts of the Muslim world to teach Muslims the Hadith.

Q.21 Mention five companions who collected Hadîth in books (Sahif)?

Ans. Abdullâh ibn Amr ibn Alas (R.Z.A.) collected 1000 sayings in a book he called "Al Sadiga". Ali collected certain laws in a book named "Al Qadaya". It is also reported that Jabir ibn Abdullâh (R.Z.A.), Abdullâh ibn Abbas (R.Z.A.) and Abu Hurairah (R.Z.A.) also collected Hadîth in books.

Q.22 When did the effort of scientifically compiling the Hadîth in books start?

Ans. In the year 101 A.H., when the Muslim empire ruler Umar ibn Abdul Aziz (R.Z.A.) instructed Muslim scholars to compile scientifically all the Prophet's (ﷺ)Hadîth.

Q.23 How did Muslim scholars go about compiling the Hadîth?

Ans. They first wrote down the rules to find out the sources of the traditions and the biographical data of the narrators. So they dealt with three subjects: the biography of the narrators with particular reference to their character and honesty, with the narration itself and with the substance of the tradition.

Q.24 How many Hadîth does the famous book "Al-Mawatta" of Imam Malik have, and on what subjects?

Ans. 1700 Hadîth, mostly on acts of devotion such as Salah, Fasting, Zakah, and Hajj.

Q.25 Mention two famous scholars of Hadîth who compiled many Hadîths carefully in their books?

Ans. Imam Bukhâri (d. 256 A.H.) who selected 2,761 Hadîth from out of 600,000 he compiled and reported them in his book Sahih-Al-Bukhâri. Imam Muslim (d. 261 A.H.) who selected 4,000 Hadîth from out of 300,000 he compiled and reported them in his book Sahih-Muslim.

Q.26 Mention four books of Hadîth which came later to Sahih-Al-Bukhâri and Sahih-Muslim?

Ans. Musnad of Abu Dawood (d. 275 A.H.), Musnad of Al-Tirmidhi

(d. 279 A.H.), Musnad of Nas'i (d. 303 A.H.) and Musnad ibn Majah (d. 295 A.H.).

Q.27 What does Isnad mean?

Ans. Each Hadîth reported in any book of Hadîth was prefaced by a chain of authorities going back to the original narrator and then the Prophet (ﷺ). This process is called Isnad.

Q.28 How have the different Hadîth been classified?

Ans. According to their degree of reliability.

Q.29 What is Hadîth Nabawi?

Ans. A saying of the Prophet (ﷺ) inspired by Allâh and given in the Prophet's (ﷺ) words.

Q.30 What is Hadîth Qudsi?

Ans. A saying of the Prophet (ﷺ) with reference to Allâh's words.

Q.31 What are the three classifications of any Hadîth according to its reliability?

Ans. Sahih (sound or most authentic) and Hassan (good or less authentic). If the Hadîth is Da-eef (weak or least authentic) it is not considered a Hadîth.

Q.32 What does Mottafaq-Alaih mean?

Ans. Hadîth which was accepted and agreed upon by both Imams Bukhâri and Muslim.

Q.33 How was the character of the narrator of the Hadîth judged?

Ans. The narrator should be a man of learning, should not have committed any crime, spoken any lie, given false evidence and should not be guilty of carelessness or indifference. His memory must be good. His religious beliefs and learning should be understood, his piety, impartiality and truthfulness must be considered.

Q.34 Mention a Hadîth to encourage planting public trees.

Ans. "A Muslim who plants a tree or sows a field, from which man, birds and animals can eat is committing an act of charity." Muslim.

Q.35 Mention a Hadîth to encourage remembrance of Allâh at all times.

Ans. "There is a polish for everything that takes away rust, the

polish for the heart is the remembrance of Allâh." Bukhâri.

Q.36 Mention a Hadîth talking about actions which are most excellent.

Ans. "What actions are most excellent? To gladden the hearts of human being; to feed the hungry, to help the afflicted, to lighten the sorrow of the sorrowful, and to remote the sufferings of the injured." Bukhâri.

Q.37 Mention a Hadîth about conquest of one's self.

Ans. "The most excellent Jihad is that for the conquest of oneself." Baihaqi.

Q.38 Mention a Hadîth regarding trust in Allâh.

Ans. "If you put your whole trust in Allâh, as you ought, He most certainly will satisfy your needs, as He satisfies those of the birds; they come out hungry in the morning, but return full to their nests." Tirmidhi.

Q.39 Mention a Hadîth regarding Allâh's compassion.

Ans. "When Allâh created his creatures, He wrote above His throne: 'Verily, my compassion overcomes my wrath." Bukhâri & Muslim.

Q.40 Mention a Hadîth regarding being merciful to anyone.

Ans. Allâh will not give mercy to anyone, except those who give mercy to other creatures." Abu Dawood & Tirmidhi.

Q.41 Mention a Hadîth regarding telling the truth.

Ans. "Say what is truth, although it may be bitter and displeasing to people." Baihaqi.

Q.42 Mention a Hadîth regarding kindness.

Ans. "Kindness is a mark of faith, and whoever is not kind has no faith." Muslim.

Q.43 Mention a Hadîth which contains a Du'â (prayer).

Ans. "O Lord, grant me your love, grant me that I love those who love you; grant me that I might do the deeds that win your love. Make your love dearer to me than the love of myself, my family and wealth." Tirmidhi.

Q.44 Mention a Hadîth regarding being in the company of people.

Ans. "It is better to sit alone, than in company with the bad; and it is better still to sit with good company than alone. It is better to

speak to a seeker of knowledge than to remain silent; but silence is better than idle words." Bukhâri.

Q.45 Mention a Hadîth regarding who are the learned.

Ans. "Who are the learned? Those who practise what they know." Bukhâri.

Q.46 Mention a Hadîth regarding serving Allâh.

Ans. "Serve Allâh as you could see Him; although you cannot see Him, He can see you." Muslim.

Q.47 Mention a Hadîth regarding loving Allâh.

Ans. "Whoever loves to meet Allâh, Allâh loves to meet him." Muslim.

Q.48 Mention a Hadîth regarding loving one another.

Ans. "You will not enter paradise until you have faith; and you will not complete your faith till you love one another." Muslim.

Q.49 Mention a Hadîth regarding the importance of Qur'ân and the Sunnah.

Ans. "I am leaving two things among you, and if you cling to them firmly you will never go astray; one is the Book of Allâh and the other is my way of life (Sunnah)." Muatta.

Q.50 Mention a Hadîth regarding the five Pillars of Islam.

Ans. "Islam has been built on five pillars: Testifying that there is no god but Allâh and that Muhammad is the Messenger of Allâh, performing the prayers, paying the Zakat, making pilgrimage to the House (Ka'ba) and fasting Ramadan." Bukhâri & Muslim.

Q.51 Mention a Hadîth regarding what is a charity.

Ans. "Every joint of every person must perform a charity everyday: to act justly between two people is a charity, to help a man with his mount, lifting him onto it or hoisting up his belonging onto, it is charity, a good word is a charity, every step you take towards a mosque is a chrity and removing a harmful thing from the road is a charity." Bukhâri & Muslim.

Q.52 Mention a Hadîth regarding our duties when we see an evil action.

Ans. "Whosoever of you sees an evil action, let him change it with hands and if he is not able, then with his tongue (by talking and

giving advice) and if he is not able, then with his heart (by offering silent prayers) and that is the weakest of faith." (*Muslim*).

Q.53 Mention a Hadîth which advises Muslims to stay away from some evil actions.

Ans. "Do not envy one another, do not inflate the prices one to another, do not hate one another and do not undercut one another." (*Muslim*).

Q.54 Mention a Hadîth which sets the rules for relations between Muslims.

Ans. "A Muslim is the brother of a Muslim; he neither oppresses him nor does he fail him (in time of need), he neither lies to him nor does he hold him in contempt." (*Muslim*).

Q.55 Mention another Hadîth which sets the rules for relations between Muslims.

Ans. "Whoever relieves a believer from a worldly grief, Allâh will relieve him from one of the grieves of the Day of Judgement. Whoever gives a lot to a needy person, Allâh will give him a lot in this world and the Hereafter. Whoever protects and shields a Muslim, Allâh will protect and shield him in this world and the Hereafter. Allâh will help and aid a worshiper as long as helps and aids his brother." (*Muslim*).

Q.56 Mention a Hadîth to encourage Muslims to seek knowledge.

Ans. "Whoever seeks a path to gain knowldge, Allâh will make easy for him a path to paradise." (*Muslim*).

Q. 57 Mention a Hadîth to encourage Muslims to read and study the Qur'ân.

Ans. "No group of people would gather in a Mosque reciting the Book of Allâh (Qur'ân) and studying it, without tranquility and peace descending upon them, mercy covering them, the angels surrounding them and Allâh is mentioning them amongst those who are with Him." (*Muslim*).

CHAPTER

3

AL-SEERA

Q. 1 Who is Muhammad (ﷺ)?

Ans. The last messenger of Allâh to humanity.

Q. 2 Where was the Prophet Muhammad (ﷺ) born?

Ans. At Mekka in Arabia.

Q. 3 In what year (A.D.) was the Prophet Muhammad (ﷺ) born?

Ans. 570 A.D.

Q. 4 What was the name given to the year in which the Prophet (ﷺ) was born?

Ans. The Year of the Elephant.

Q. 5 Why was the year the Prophet (ﷺ) was born called the Year of the Elephant?

Ans. Because of the attempt to destroy the Ka'ba with an army using elehants.

Q. 6 Name the Prophet's (ﷺ) father?

Ans. Abdullâh.

Q. 7 Who named the Prophet "Muhammad" (ﷺ)?

Ans. His grandfather.

Q. 8 What is the meaning of the name "Muhammad (ﷺ)"?

Ans. The praised one.

Q. 9 In what year (A.D.) was the Prophet's (ﷺ) father born?

Ans. 545 A.D.

Q.10 Name the Prophet's (ﷺ) grandfather.

Ans. Abdul Muttalib.

Q.11 Name the Prophet's (ﷺ) great-grandfather.

Ans. Hashim.

Q.12 Name the Prophet's (ﷺ) great-great-grandfather.

Ans. Abd Manaf.

Q.13 Name the Prophet's (ﷺ) mother.

Ans. Âmna, the daughter of Wahab.

Q.14 The Prophet's (ﷺ) father died before his birth. True or false.

Yes. True.

Q.15 In what year (A.D.) did the Prophet's (ﷺ) mother die?

Ans. 575 A.D.

Q.16 How old was the Prophet (ﷺ) when his mother died?

Ans. About 6 years old.

Q.17 How did the people of Mekka treat our Prophet (ﷺ) before he announced his Prophethood?

Ans. They had great regard, honour and respect for him. He was named the trustworthy (Al-ameen).

Q.18 What is Al Hijra?

Ans. The migration of our Prophet (ﷺ) from Mekka to Medina.

Q.19 When did the Prophet (ﷺ) migrate?

Ans. Thirteen (13) years after calling the people of Mekka to Islam.

Q.20 How old was the Prophet (ﷺ) when he died?

Ans. He died at the age of sixty-three years.

Q.21 Should we visit the Prophet's (ﷺ) Mosque where he was buried?

Ans. Yes, preferable after the performance of Hajj (pilgrimage) to Mekka.

Q.22 What is the name of the Prophet's (ﷺ) tribe?

Ans. Quraish.

Q.23 How many children did Abdul-Muttalib have?

Ans. Ten.

Q.24 What is the name of the youngest son of Abdul-Muttalib?

Ans. Abdullâh, the father of the Prophet Muhammad (ﷺ).

Q.25 What was the sad event that happened shortly after Âmna became pregnant with the Prophet (ﷺ)?

Ans. Her husband, Abdullah died on a trading trip.

Q.26 Where was Abdullâh, the father of Muhammad (ﷺ) buried?

Ans. In Medina.

Q.27 What was the most important characteristic of the Prophet (ﷺ) as he grew up?

Ans. He was honest. He was called Al-ameen (the trustworthy).

Q.28 What was the name of our Prophet's (ﷺ) first wife?

Ans. Khadeejah.

Q.29 How old was the Prophet (ﷺ) when he married Khadeejah?

Ans. Twenty-five.

Q.30 Who took care of the Prophet (ﷺ) after his mother's death?

Ans. His grandfather, Abdul Muttalib.

Q.31 In what year (A.D.) did the the Prophet's (ﷺ) grandfather die?

Ans. 578 A.D.

Q.32 Who took care of the Prophet (ﷺ) after his grandfather's death?

Ans. His uncle, Abu Talib.

Q.33 How was the Prophet Muhammad (ﷺ) educated?

Ans. He did not receive any formal or informal education through human agency, so he did not know how to read or write.

Q.34 What did the Prophet (ﷺ) do to earn his living as a young man?

Ans. He was a shepherd and a trader.

Q.35 How old was the Prophet (ﷺ) when Allâh's first message of Qur'ân revealed to him?

Ans. When he was forty years old.

Q.36 Where was Allâh's first message of Qur'ân revealed to the Prophet Muhammad (ﷺ)?

Ans. At a cave at the foot of Mount Hira' in Mekka.

Q.37 Who revealed Allâh's first message of the Qur'ân and subsequent messages to the Prophet (ﷺ)?

Ans. The Angel Gabriel.

Q.38 For how long was the Prophet (ﷺ) married to Khadeejah?

Ans. For twenty-six years.

Q.39 How old was the Prophet (ﷺ) when his wife Khadeejah died?

Ans. When she died he was fifty-one years old.

Q.40 How many children did the Prophet (ﷺ) and Khadeejah have?

Ans. Seven children.

Q.41 How many sons and daughters did the Prophet (ﷺ) have from Khadeejah (R.Z.A.)?

Ans. He had three sons and four daughters.

Q.42 Name the Prophet's (ﷺ) sons from Khadeejah.

Ans. Al-Kasem, Al-Tayeb, Al-Taher.

Q.43 Name the Prophet's (ﷺ) daughters from Khadeejah.

Ans. Ruqaiyah (R.Z.A.), Zynab (R.Z.A.), Umm Kulthum (R.Z.A.), and Fatima (R.Z.A.).

Q.44 All the Prophet's (ﷺ) children from Khadeejah died before him, except for Fatima (R.Z.A.). True or False.

Ans. True.

Q.45 What did the Arabs believe in, before Islam?

Ans. They were Idolators.

Q.46 Did the Prophet Muhammad (ﷺ) join the Arabs before Allâh's revelation to him, in their worship of idols and in drinking and gambling?

Ans. No. Instead he used to go up to the mountain cave and stay there.

Q.47 What happened to the Prophet (ﷺ) when he was at the cave one time?

Ans. The angel Gabriel appeared to him and said, "Read". The Prophet said "I cannot read.". The angel hugged him and said, "Read.". The Prophet (ﷺ) said, "I cannot read". For the third time the angel held him and said, "Read" "and the Prophet (ﷺ) answered, "I cannot read.". Before disappearing the angel said, "Read in the name of your Lord Who created man from a clot of blood. Read for your Lord is the most bountiful, Who taught man (the use of) the pen, He taught man which he knew not".

Q.48 How old was the Prophet (ﷺ) when the angel Gabriel came to him?

Ans. Forty, and from that time he became the last Prophet of Allâh.

Q.49 What did the Prophet (ﷺ) do after the first revelation from the angel Gabriel?

Ans. He hurried down the hillside of Mount Hira and reached home tired and frightened and asked Khadeejah, "Wrap me up, wrap me up." and then he told her what had happened.

Q.50 What did Khadeejah answer after the Prophet (ﷺ) told her of the first revelation?

Ans. "Allâh will not let you down. You are kind to relatives. You speak only the truth. You help the poor, the orphans and the needy. You are a good man."

Q.51 To whom did the Prophet (ﷺ) preach Islam first?

Ans. To his family and friends secretly.

Q.52 Who were the first to accept Islam?

Ans. His wife Khadeejah (R.Z.A.), his cousin Ali, his servant Zayd ibn Harithah (R.Z.A.); his friend Abu Bakr (R.Z.A.), and Abu Bakr's (R.Z.A.) daughters and wife.

Q.53 How many people accepted Islam after three years of preaching?

Ans. Only forty. After these three years. Allâh ordered the Prophet (ﷺ) to start preaching Islam in the open to everyone.

Q.54 How did people react to the Prophet (ﷺ) when he started to preach Islam openly?

Ans. With hostility. They called him names. They did not believe his words. They said if Allâh wanted to send a messenger he would have sent an angel. Muhammad (ﷺ) was just a man. They called him a fortuneteller, but they knew he really wasn't. They said he was making up poems, but they had never heard poems like these. They called him mad, but they knew he had never acted mad before. They called him a liar, but they knew that they themselves called him the honest one.

Q.55 Who was the closest to the Prophet (ﷺ) and one of the most hostile?

Ans. His uncle Abu Lahab and his wife.

Q.56 How did the people try to tempt the Prophet (ﷺ) to stop preaching Islam.

Ans. By offering him money, power and to be their king.

Q.57 How did people try to pressure his uncle to stop supporting the Prophet (ﷺ)?

Ans. They offered to kill Muhmmad (ﷺ) in return for his uncle adopting one of the best to their men.

Q.58 What was the Prophet's (ﷺ) answer when his uncle asked him to stop preaching Islam?

Ans. "Uncle, if they were to put the sun in my right hand and the moon in my left hand to stop me from preaching Islam, I would never stop. I will keep preaching until Allâh makes Islam prevail or until I die."

Q.59 How did the non-believers treat the believers?

Ans. Badly. The believers were beaten, tortured and lost their business.

Q.60 Who was the first martyr (died for their belief) in Islam?

Ans. The mother of Ammar ibn Yasir (R.Z.A.).

Q.61 What did the Prophet (ﷺ) do when the Muslims suffering increased greatly?

Ans. He sent most of them to Abyssinia in Africa, whose king was a Christian.

Q.62 What did the disbelievers do when some Muslims went to Abyssinia?

Ans. They sent presents to the king of Abyssinia, asking him to send the Muslims back to Arabia. The king refused and later became a Muslim.

Q.63 What was the name of the king of Abyssinia?

Ans. As-a-ma (Elnagashy).

Q.64 Who was the important person who accepted Islam shortly after the migration to Abyssinia?

Ans. Umar ibn Al-Khattab (R.Z.A.), a wise and a strong man.

Q.65 What was the sad event which happened at the tenth year of the Prophethood?

Ans. Abu Talib, the Prophet's (ﷺ) uncle and Khadeejah (R.Z.A.), the Prophet's (ﷺ) wife, both died.

Q.66 What happened after the death of Abu Talib and Khadeejah (R.Z.A.)?

Ans. The cruel treatment of the Prophet (ﷺ) and the Muslims increased greatly.

Q.67 What did the Prophet (ﷺ) do after the death of Abu Talib and Khadeejah (R.Z.A.)?

Ans. He asked the protection of the people of Taif, near Mekka, but they refused and made fun of him.

Q.68 What is Al-Isra'?

Ans. The trip where Allâh took the Prophet (ﷺ) from the sacred mosque in Mecca to the spot where the Al-Aqsa mosque is, in Jerusalem, in a very short time of one night.

Q.69 What is Al-Mi-râg?

Ans. The trip where Allâh took the Prophet (ﷺ) after Al-Isra' to the heavens.

Q.70 Did the nonbelievers believe the Prophet (ﷺ) (when he told them about the Al-Isra'and Al-Mirâg?

Ans. No. They said, "How can you go to Jerusalem and back, which takes a month by camel, in one night. Yet you say also you went to the heavens."

Q.71 When do Muslims celebrate the occasion of Al-Isra-a and Al-Mirâg?

Ans. On the 27th of Rajab; the seventh month of the Islâmic (lunar) calender.

Q.72 What did the Prophet (ﷺ) say to the non-believers when they did not believe him about Al-Isra'?

Ans. He told them about Jerusalem and about caravans he saw coming back from Jerusalem towards Mecca.

Q.73 What is the old name of the City of Al-Medina (means The City)?

Ans. Yathrib.

Q.74 Who used to live in Al-Medina before the Muslims immigrated there?

Ans. Jews and two Arab tribes, Al-Aws and Al-Khazraj.

Q.75 What was the situation in Al-Medina before the Muslims arrived?

Ans. The two Arab tribes were fighting each other and the Jews helping both sides.

Q.76 What was the first pledge of Al-Aqabah?

Ans. Twelve men from Yathrib came to Mekka and promised the Prophet (ﷺ) not to associate anything with Allâh, not to steal, not to commit adultery, not to kill their children, not to slander and not to disobey Allâh.

Q.77 How was Islam introduced to Yathrib?

Ans. Through the twelve men who made the pledge near Mecca

with the Prophet (ﷺ) and through Musʻab ibn Uma-eer, who the Prophet sent back with them.

Q.78 What was the second pledge of Al-Aqabah?

Ans. One year after the first pledge, 75 Muslims left Yathrib for Mekka and their leader promised the Prophet (ﷺ) that they would defend the Prophet (ﷺ) and his followers as they defend their families if they join them in Yathrib.

Q.79 What did the Prophet (ﷺ) instruct the Muslims of Mekka to do after the second pledge of Al-Aqabah?

Ans. He ordered them to go to Yathrib secretly, alone or in small groups.

Q.80 What did the nobelievers do to the Prophet (ﷺ) after most of the Muslims left Mecca?

Ans. They plotted to kill him. Each tribe chose one strong man and all of the men were sent to stab the Prophet (ﷺ) at the same time, so that the Prophet's (ﷺ) tribe would not be able to punish anyone.

Q.81 Did the Prophet (ﷺ) learn about the plot to kill him?

Ans. Yes. He learned of the plot from Allâh. Allâh asked the Prophet (ﷺ) to leave for Yathrib.

Q.82 How did the Prophet (ﷺ) leave Mekka?

Ans. The Prophet (ﷺ) told Abu Bakr (R.Z.A.), one of his companions about the plot and Allâh's order to leave Mekka and asked him to get ready to leave for Yathrib. The Prophet (ﷺ) told Ali (R.Z.A.), the Prophet's (ﷺ) cousin and one of his companions, of his plan and asked him to lay on the Prophet's (ﷺ) bed to mislead his enemies, knowing that Allâh would protect Ali (R.Z.A.). The non-believers came to the Prophet's (ﷺ) house at night and waited for him to come out, but they got sleepy. The Prophet (ﷺ) quietly left his house. No one could see him. He went to Abu Bakr (R.Z.A.). Together they rode south instead of going north towards Yathrib. The nonbelievers at the Prophet's (ﷺ) house got suspicious and went in. They found Ali (R.Z.A.) and ran out to search for the Prophet (ﷺ). The Prophet (ﷺ) and Abu Bakr (R.Z.A.) hid in a cave at a mountain called Thawr. The non-believers came near the cave. The Prophet (ﷺ) told Abu Bakr (R.Z.A.), "Do not be afraid, for Allâh is with us." and the searchers could not see them. Three days later, the Prophet (ﷺ) and Abu Bakr (R.Z.A.) left for Yathrib.

Q.83 Did the non-believers continue the search for the Prophet (ﷺ) after he left for Yathrib?

Ans. Yes, a reward of 100 camels was offered for capturing the Prophet (ﷺ), dead or alive. Even when the Prophet (ﷺ) and Abu Bakr (R.Z.A.) took an uncommon route to Yathrib, one of the non-believers found their tracks. As he got near them, his horse threw him to ground. He accepted Islam then, and did not harm the Prophet (ﷺ) or Abu Bakr (R.Z.A.).

Q.84 What is the name of the village outside Yathrib where the Prophet (ﷺ) stayed in for four days and build the first Mosque in Islam?

Ans. Qoba'.

Q.85 How did Muslims of Yathrib greet the Prophet (ﷺ)?

Ans. Men, women, boys and girls were out to meet him, they were singing and everyone hoped that the Prophet (ﷺ) would stay with them.

Q.86 What did the Prophet (ﷺ) say to the Muslims of Yathrib, regarding where he would stay?

Ans. He said that his camel is guided by Allâh and the place where it kneels down would be the place where his home will be. It stopped in an open space belonging to two orphan brothers. The Prophet (ﷺ) bought it from them and built his house and a Mosque.

Q.87 What was the first thing the Prophet (ﷺ) did in Yathrib?

Ans. He asked each Muslim from Yathrib to take a brother, one of the Muslims of Mekka, and treat him as family.

Q.88 What did the Prophet (ﷺ) do in Yathrib?

Ans. He called people to Islam. Many Arab tribes accepted Islam, also some Jews and Christians. He also sent messengers to many countries calling them to Islam: Heraclius of the Roman Empire, Kesra (emperor) of the Persian Empire, the governor of Egypt and the King of Yemen.

Q.89 What was the first battle between the Muslims of Yathrib and the non-believers of Mecca?

Ans. The battle of Badr.

Q.90 When was the battle of Badr?

Ans. It happened on the 17th of Ramadan, the second year after Hajra (immigration of the Muslims to Yathrib).

Q.91 What led to the battle of Badr?

Ans. The non-believers were being cruel to the Muslims. They forced them to leave Mecca. Moreover, the non-believers took everything the Muslims left behind in Mecca. One day, the Prophet (ﷺ) heard of a caravan of Quraysh (one of the tribes of Mekka) leaving Mekka for Syria. The Muslims, led by the Prophet (ﷺ) went to seize the caravan in its way back to Mekka. They went too late as the caravan had already passed. Later, the non-believers of Mekka gathered their army; 1000 men, 7 camels, and 100 horses, and went out to protect their caravan. However the caravan, led by Abu Sufyan (R.Z.A.) changed route and returned safely to Mekka. But the non-believers' army went on to teach the Muslims a lesson. The Muslim army had 305 men, 70 camels and 5 horses. The two armies met at Badr. The Muslims took the victory.

Q.92 How did the Jews of Madina (Yathrib) look upon the battle of Badr?

Ans. They thought the Muslims would lose. They also sided with Quraish of Mekka and told Quraish that they should take revenge.

Q.93 What was the first incident between the Muslims and the Jews?

Ans. One Jew of the Jewish tribe of Bani Qaynaqa' attacked a Muslim woman while she was walking through their village. A Muslim man saw the attack and rushed to help her. The Jews were too many and beat the man to death. The Muslims attacked the village and for 15 days they laid siege to the village of Bani Qaynaqa'. The Jews surrendered and went into exile.

Q.94 What did the non-believers do at Mekka after the battle of Badr?

Ans. They prepared a strong army of 3000 men to take revenge.

Q.95 What and when was the second battle between the Muslims and the non-believers?

Ans. The battle of Uhud which happened in the month of Shawal, one year after the battle of Badr.

Q.96 What did the Muslims do when they heard about the non believers' army at the battle of Uhud?

Ans. They decided to meet the non-believers' army outside Medina, five kilometers north of the city at a mountain called Uhud.

Q.97 What important instructions did the Prophet (ﷺ) give his army in the battle of Uhud?

Ans. He asked fifty archers to station on the mountain of Uhud, to protect the Muslim army from behind, and not to leave their place even if the Muslims win.

Q.98 What hapened at the beginning of the battle of Uhud?

Ans. The Muslims were winning. The non-believers' army fled, leaving their belongings and some of the archers left their places thinking that the battle was over.

Q.99 How did the battle of Uhud turn around?

Ans. Khalid ibn-Al-Walîd (R.Z.A.), then the leader of the non-believers' horsemen saw the archers leave their posts. He attacked the Muslim army and caught them by surprise. Their victory soon became a defeat.

Q.100 How did the non believers carry the battle of Uhud further?

Ans. They shouted that the Prophet (ﷺ) had been killed to lower the morale of the Muslim army. They then tried to kill the Prophet (ﷺ). But the Muslims protected him and seven of them were killed.

Q.101 What was the outcome of the battle of Uhud?

Ans. The non-believers won the battle. The Muslims had seventy martyrs defending Islam. One of them was the Prophet's (ﷺ) uncle, Hamzah ibn Abdul-Muttalib (R.Z.A.).

Q.102 What was the Jews of Medina's reaction to the outcome of the battle of Uhud?

Ans. They were happy. They said "If Muhmmad (ﷺ) was really a Prophet (ﷺ), he would not have lost."

Q.103 What were the Jewish tribes which were left in Medina?

Ans. Bani Al-Nadhir and Bani Quraidhah. Bani Qaynaqa' had left Medina after the battle of Badr.

Q.104 How did the Jewish tribes treat the Prophet (ﷺ)?

Ans. Many among Bani Al-Nadhir wanted to kill him. One man went up to the top of a wall and tried to drop a large stone on the Prophet (ﷺ) but he moved and the stone missed him.

Q.105 How did the Muslims react to the Bani Al-Nadir attempt to kill the Prophet (ﷺ)?

Ans. They fought them for 20 days until they surrendered and left Medina. Only the Jewish tribe of Bani Quraydhah was left in Medina.

Q.106 What did the non-believers do after the battle of Uhud?

Ans. They were putting together an even stronger army to attack Medina.

Q.107 What and when was the third battle between Muslims and the non-believers?

Ans. The battle of the trench (Al Khandek) in the month of Shawal, two years after the battle of Uhud (5 A.H.).

Q.108 How did the battle of the trench progress?

Ans. One of the Muslims, Salman Al-Farisi (R.Z.A.), suggested that the Muslims stay in Medina and dig a trench to protect themselves. The Muslims dug the trench at the north end of the city. The east and the west sides of the city were rocky and the non-believers would not come from those sides. The Muslims had also made a treaty with the Jewish tribe of Bani Quraidhah, who had a fortress at the south end, to protect the city from the south.

Q.109 Did the Jewish tribe of Bani Quraidhah break the treaty with the Muslims?

Ans. Yes, The Muslim army was then in real danger, but their morale was very high. The battle went on across the trench.

Q.110 What was the outcome ot the battle of the trench?

Ans. Allâh caused a strong, cold, bitter wind to sweep over the army of the non-believers, almost a month after the siege had started. The non-believers' army, led by Abu Sufyan (R.Z.A.), then non believer retreated to Mekka.

Q.111 What did the Muslims do to Bani Quraydhah?

Ans. Because they broke the treaty, the Muslims fought them for twenty-five days and won.

Q.112 What happened in the year 6 A.H., one year after the battle of the trench?

Ans. The Prophet (ﷺ) took the Muslims to Mecca for Hajj with no arms. Near Mecca, they stopped at a place called Hudaybiyah for a final rest. Quraish asked for a treaty with the Muslims. The Muslims were not to visit Mecca until the following year and both sides would not make war against each other for ten years.

Q.113 Did Quraish break the Hudaibiyah treaty?

Ans. Yes. Quraish helped the Arab tribe of Bani Bakr against the tribe of Bani Khuza'ah, who were allies of the Muslims. This was against the treaty.

Q.114 What did the Muslims do after the break of the Hudaibiyah treat?

Ans. On the 10th of Ramadan, 8 A.H., the Prophet (ﷺ) marched to Mecca with 10,000 Muslims.

Q.115 What happened on the way to Mecca after the breaking of the Hudaibiyah treaty?

Ans. The Prophet (ﷺ) asked the army to set up camp and light many campfires. Abu Sufyan (R.Z.A.) then non believer saw the campfires and he and two others from Mekka came to see what was going on. They were captured by the Muslim army. Abu Sufyan was stunned by the treatment he received by his enemy, he expected to be tortured or killed. With the treatment he received, he knew he was wrong and accepted Islam in front of the Prophet (ﷺ).

Q.116 What did Abu Sufyan (R.Z.A.) do after accepting Islam?

Ans. He went back to Mekka and told his people that Muhammad (ﷺ) and his army were coming and that the Prophet (ﷺ) had said whoever entered Abu Sufyan's (R.Z.A.) house would be safe, Whoever shut his door would be safe, and whoever laid down his arms would be safe.

Q.117 Was there any battle as the Muslim army entered Mecca?

Ans. No. On the 20th of Ramadan, 8 A.H., the army entered Mecca with no fighting.

Q.118 What did the Prophet (ﷺ) do after he entered Mecca in 8 A.H.?

Ans. He ordered all the idols be destroyed around Ka'ba and told the people of Mecca, "Go your way, for you are free.", and he asked Bilal (R.Z.A.) to say the Azan (call for prayer) from the top of the Ka'ba.

Q.119 Did the Prophet (ﷺ) stay in Mecca after the Muslim army entered Mecca?

Ans. No, he returned to Medina.

Q.120 What important event happened in 10 A.H.?

Ans. The Prophet (ﷺ) went for Hajj in Mecca with about 100,000 Muslims and gave the farewell sermon (Khutbah) at the plains of Mount Arafat.

Q.121 What was the most important message in the Prophet's (ﷺ) last Khutbah?

Ans. "People, I am leaving you two things as guidance. You will not go wrong as long as you follow them. They are the Book of Allâh (the Qur'ân) and the Sunnah (teachings) of His messenger."

Q.122 What was Allâh's last revelation during the farewell pilgrimage?

Ans. "This day I (Allâh) have completed your religion and completed My blessing to you and have chosen Islam as your religion.", 5:3.

Q.123 When and where did the Prophet (ﷺ) pass away?

Ans. On Monday, 12 Rabi-Al-Awal, 11 A.H., at the age of 63, in Medina.

Q.124 **How did the Prophet's (ﷺ) companions react to his death?**

Ans. They were shocked. Abu Bakr (R.Z.A.) said to his people, "If any of you worshipped Muhammad (ﷺ), he is now dead, and if any of you worship Allâh, He is alive and will never die and read from Qur'ân: "Muhammad (ﷺ) is no more than a messenger, other messengers have passed away before him. If he dies or if he is killed, will you become non-believers? He who becomes a non believer will do no harm to Allâh. Allâh will reward the thankful.", 3:144.

Q.125 **Where was the Prophet (ﷺ) buried?**

Ans. In the same spot where he died, the house of his wife 'Aysha (R.Z.A.), the daughter of Abu Bakr (R.Z.A.). The house was near his Mosque Medina. Today the Prophet's (ﷺ) grave is inside the Mosque. The Mosque has been made larger over the years, until it covered the house in which he died.

CHAPTER 4

AL-IMAN

Q. 1 Who created you and the Universe?
Ans. Allâh.

Q. 2 What is your first duty to Allâh?
Ans. To believe in Him and submit completely to His commands.

Q. 3 How do you acquire knowledge about Allâh and His commands?
Ans. Through the Qur'ân and the Traditions of the Last Prophet Muhammad.

Q. 4 What is the Qur'ân?
Ans. The Holy Book of Allâh revealed to the Prophet Muhammad (ﷺ) through the Angel Gabriel (A.S.).

Q. 5 What are the traditions of the Prophet Muhammad (ﷺ)?
Ans. The Prophet's (ﷺ) sayings, deeds and approvals of certain actions.

Q. 6 What is a Prophet (ﷺ)?
Ans. A very special and pious man chosen by Allâh to convey His commands.

Q. 7 Who did Allâh send at different times, when people went astray to guide them?
Ans. Prophets (ﷺ) and Messengers.

Q. 8 The message of the Prophet Muhammad (ﷺ) is called the Religion of Islam, what does Islam mean?
Ans. The complete submission to the will of Allâh.

Q. 9 What are the six articles of faith in Islam?
Ans. To believe in the oneness of Allâh, His Angels, His books, His

Prophets (ﷺ), the Day of Judgement, and that the power of doing all actions (good or bad) is from Allâh.

Q.10 What are the five fundamental pillars of Islam?

Ans. To testify that there is no god worthy of worship but Allâh, and that Muhammad (ﷺ) is the Messenger of Allâh, to establish regularly the five daily prayers, to distribute the Zakah once a year among the deserving, to fast during the day time in the month of Ramadan, to perform the pilgrimage if capable.

Q.11 Does Allâh know all the actions and thoughts of everyone?

Ans. Yes.

Q.12 How do you gain the favour and the love of Allâh?

Ans. By complete submission to His commands.

Q.13 What does faith (Iman) mean?

Ans. To believe.

Q.14 Is faith sufficient to receive Allâh's blessings?

Ans. No. Faith without doing good deeds is as insufficient as doing good deeds without faith.

Q.15 What kind of creatures are the Angels?

Ans. They are created from light and have the ability to change their appearance and are forever obedient to Allâh.

Q.16 Name some Angels, as mentioned in the Qur'ân or Sunnah.

Ans. Jibra'îl (A.S.) (Gabriel), Mika'îl (A.S.), Israfîl (A.S.), Izra'îl (A.S.), Mâlik (A.S.).

Q.17 What are the duties of the Angel Jibra'îl (A.S.)?

Ans. He is the intermediary of Allâh to the Prophets (ﷺ) to inform them about the instructions of Allâh.

Q.18 What are the duties of the Angel Mika'îl (A.S.)?

Ans. He is the Angel in charge of sustaince and rain.

Q.19 What are the duties of the Angel Israfîl (A.S.)?

Ans. He is the Angel who will blow the horn on the day of Resurrection.

Q.20 What is the other name of Izra'îl (A.S.)?
Ans. Malak-ul-Maut, (Angel of death).

Q.21 What are the duties of Izra'îl (A.S.)?
Ans. He is the Angel of Death.

Q.22 What are the duties of Mâlik (A.S.)?
Ans. He is the Angel in charge of Hell.

Q.23 What are the duties of the Angel Ridhwan (A.S.)?
Ans. He is the Angel in charge of Paradise.

Q.24 People are questioned in the grave by two Angels. True or false.
Ans. True.

Q.25 What are the duties of the Zabania?
Ans. They are the assistants of the Angel Mâlik (A.S.).

Q.26 What is the name of the Angels which carry the throne of Allâh?
Ans. Hamalâtul' Arsh.

Q.27 What are the Angels around the throne of Allâh called?
Ans. Al-Mukarrabîn.

Q.28 What are the Angels who write the deeds of everybody called?
Ans. Al-Katabah.

Q.29 There is an angel on your right who is responsible to write your good deeds. True or false.
Ans. True.

Q.30 There is an angel on your left who is responsible to write your bad deeds. True or false.
Ans. True.

Q.31 What are the Angels who protect everyone called?
Ans. The Hafaza.

Q.32 What is the word angel in Arabic?
Ans. Malak.

Q.33 Can Angels do anything without the permission of Allâh?
Ans. No.

Q.34 Are you allowed to worship Angels?
Ans. No.

Q.35 Name the revelations to the Prophet Ibrahim (A.S.).
Ans. Souhouf Ibrahim (A.S.).

Q.36 Name the revelations to the Prophet Dawûd (A.S.).
Ans. Zabûr (part of the Psalms).

Q.37 Name the book revealed to the Prophet Mûsâ (A.S.) (Moses)?
Ans. The Tourâh (Torah, part of the Old Testament).

Q.38 Name the book revealed to the Prophet 'Îsa (A.S.) (Jesus).
Ans. The Injîl (part of the New Testament).

Q.39 Name the book revealed to our Prophet Muhammad (ﷺ)?
Ans. The Qur'ân.

Q.40 Which Book of Revelation is the only book which is still Intact today as it was revealed to that Prophet (ﷺ)?
Ans. The Qur'ân.

Q.41 Are other Books of Revelations, other than the Qur'ân still in their original language and form today as they were revealed?
Ans. No.

Q.42 What do you mean by belief in all Allâh's Prophets (ﷺ)?
Ans. To believe in the Prophets (ﷺ) referred to in the Qur'ân, but no others.

Q.43 Does the Qur'ân mention all the names of Allâh's Prophet's (ﷺ)?
Ans. No, only some are mentioned by name. Allâh, in the Qur'ân, tells us that there are others.

Q.44 Who was the first Prophet (ﷺ) of Allâh?
Ans. Adam (A.S.).

Q.45 What was the message given to Adam (A.S.) by Allâh?

Ans. The message of Islam (total submission to Allâh's commands).

Q.46 Mention four names of Prophets (ﷺ) chosen by Allâh after Adam (A.S.) and before Ibrahim (A.S.)?

Ans. Idrîs (A.S.), Nûh (A.S.), Hûd (A.S.), Sâleh (A.S.).

Q.47 Mention the names of the two Prophets who were the sons of Ibrahim (A.S.)?

Ans. Ismâ'îl (A.S.) (Ishmael) and Ishâq (A.S.) (Isaq).

Q.48 Who is the Prophet who was at the same time as the Prophet Ibrâhim (A.S.)?

Ans. Lût (A.S.) (Lot).

Q.49 Who is the Prophet who was at the same time as the Prophet Mûsâ (A.S.) (Moses)?

Ans. His brother Harûn (A.S.) (Aaron).

Q.50 Who are the two Prophets who were at the same time as the Prophet 'Îsa (A.S.) (Jesus)?

Ans. Zakâria (A.S.) (Zacharias) and Yahya (A.S.) (John the Baptist).

Q.51 Can any of the Prophets be called Gods or Sons of God?

Ans. No. Prophets are created by God (Allâh).

Q.52 Did any of the Prophets claim to be God?

Ans. No. They all are messengers of God and servants to Him.

Q.53 To what nation was the Prophet Muhammad (ﷺ) sent?

Ans. To all nations, to mankind.

Q.54 Will there be any Prophet after the Prophet Muhammad (ﷺ)?

Ans. No, Allâh in the Holy Qur'ân, says that the Prophet Muhammad (ﷺ) is the last and "the seal of all Prophets and Messengers"

Q.55 What is the Day of Resurrection and Judgement?

Ans. The day Allâh will make the dead alive again. The day Allâh will judge each person according to his or her deeds during this worldly life.

Q.56 What will happen after the judgement on the Day of Judgement?

Ans. If the person's actions were in accord to Allâh's commands, he or she will be sent to Heaven and if they are not according to Allâh's commands, he or she will be sent to Hell.

Q.57 What is Heaven?

Ans. A place of peace and happiness, where every wish is fulfilled.

Q.58 What is Hell?

Ans. A place of torture, pain and agony.

Q.59 What is a sin?

Ans. Any action against the commands of Allâh as stated in the Qur'ân and in the practices of the Prophet.

Q.60 Who can forgive sins?

Ans. Allâh and Allâh alone.

Q.61 What should you do so Allâh may forgive your sins?

Ans. Resolve never to commit any such sin and ask Allâh and Allâh alone for forgiveness.

Q.62 Can you name the most major sin of all?

Ans. Not to believe in Allâh and to believe in anyone as partner to Allâh.

Q.63 Name 10 major sins.

Ans. To disbelieve in Allâh, His Prophets, His Books, His angels, The Day of Judgement, to lie, to commit adultery, to kill, to rob or steal, to cheat, to drink alcohol or take drugs, to eat pork or its products, to neglect to do any acts of worship (praying, fasting, Zakah and Hajj), to backbite and to bear false witness.

Q.64 What are the Asma-Allâh-Al-Husna?

Ans. Attributes (names) of Allâh which are mentioned in the Qur'ân and Sunnah.

Q.65 How many Asma-Allâh-Al-Husna are there?

Ans. 99

Q.66 Mention four of the Asma-Allâh-Al-Husna which are mentioned in the first Sûrah (Al-Fatiha).

Ans. Allâh, Al-Rahman, Al-Rahîm and Al-Ma-lek.

Q.67 What is the meaning of Al-Rahman?

Ans. The Compassionate, the Beneficent.

Q.68 What is the meaning of Al-Rahîm?

Ans. The Most Merciful, Most Gracious.

Q.69 What is the meaning of Al-Ma-lek?

Ans. The Possessor of all, the Sovereign.

Q.70 Mention one of the Asma-Allâh-Al-Husna which is mentioned in Sûrah Al-Nâs (114).

Ans. Ma-lek.

Q.71 What is the meaning of Ma-lek?

Ans. The King.

Q.72 Mention two of the Asma-Allâh-Al-Husna which are mentioned in Sûrah Al-Ikhlâs (112)

Ans. Al-Ahed (meaning Al-Wâhid), Al-Samad.

Q.73 What is the meaning of Al-Wâhid?

Ans. The One.

Q.74 What is the meaning of Al-Samad?

Ans. He on Whom all depend.

Q.75 How many Asma-Allâh-Al-Husna are mentioned in the last two verses of Sûrah Al-Hashr (59)?

Ans. 17

Q.76 What is the meaning of Al-Quddûs mentioned in the last two verses of Sûrah Al-Hashr (59)?

Ans. The Most Holy, the Most Pure, the Most Perfect.

Q.77 What is the meaning of Al-Salâm mentioned in the last two verses of Sûrah Al-Hashr (59)?

Ans. The Source of Peace, Safety, and Well-Being.

Q.78 What is the meaning of Al-Mu'min mentioned in the last two verses of Sûrah Al-Hashr (59)?

Ans. The Guardian of faith, Giver of Security.

Q.79 What is the meaning of Al-Muhaimin mentioned in the last two verses of Sûrah Al-Hashr (59)?

Ans. The Guardian, the Master.

Q.80 What is the meaning of Al-Aziz mentioned in the last two verses of Sûrah Al-Hashr (59)?

Ans. The Mighty, Most Strong, Most Powerful, Most Respected, Most Noble, Most Beloved.

Q.81 What is the meaning of Al-Jabbâr mentioned in the last two verses of Sûrah Al-Hashr (59)?

Ans. The Most Supreme, Almighty.

Q.82 What is the meaning of Al-Mutakabbir mentioned in the last two verses of Sûrah Al-Hashr (59)?

Ans. The Possessor of every greatness, Majestic.

Q.83 What is the meaning of Al-Khâliq mentioned in the last verse of Sûrah Al-Hashr (59)?

Ans. The Creator, Originator.

Q.84 What is the meaning of Al-Bâri mentioned in the last verse of Sûrah Al-Hashr (59)?

Ans. The Perfect Maker from nothing.

Q.85 What is the meaning of Al-Musawir mentioned in the last verse of Sûrah Al-Hashr (59)?

Ans. The Perfect Fashioner, Shaper, Bestower of Forms.

Q.86 What is the meaning of Al-Hakîm mentioned in the last verse of Sûrah Al-Hashr (59)?

Ans. The Most Wise, Judicious.

Q.87 What is the meaning of Al-Ghaffar mentioned in 20:82?

Ans. The Most Forgiver, Pardoner.

Q.88 What is the meaning of Al-Qahar mentioned in 14:48?

Ans. The Most Dominant, the Conqueror, Supreme.

Q.89 What is the meaning of Al-Wahâb mentioned in 3:8?
Ans. The Most Generous Giver.

Q.90 What is the meaning of Al-Razzaq mentioned in 51:58?
Ans. The Provider, the Bestower of sustenance.

Q.91 What is the meaning of Al-Fattah mentioned in 34:26?
Ans. The Greatest of Judge, Granter of Success, Victory, Mercy and Knowledge.

Q.92 What is the meaning of Al-Alim mentioned in 34:26?
Ans. The All-Knowing.

Q.93 What are the meanings of Al-Qâbed and Al-Bâsit mentioned (in the verb form rather than the noun) in 2:245?
Ans. The Restrainer, Constrainer, Withholder.
The Spreader, Extender, Embracer.

Q.94 What are the meaning of Al-Khafid and Al-Rafi' referred to indirectly in 56:3?
Ans. The Humilator.
The Upraiser.

Q.95 What are the meanings of Al-Mu'iz and Al-Muzil mentioned (in the verb form rather than the noun) in 3:26?
Ans. The Honour.
The Degrader.

Q.96 What are the meanings of Al-Sami' and Al-Basîr mentioned in 17:1?
Ans. The All-Hearer.
The All-Seer.

Q.97 What is the meaning of Al-Ha-kimm mentioned in 10:109?
Ans. The Judge, the Giver of True Justice, the Arbitrator.

Q.98 What is the meaning of Al-'Adl mentioned indirectly in 4:58?
Ans. The Just, the Impartial, the Equitable.

Q.99 What is the meaning of Al-Latîf mentioned in 6:103?
Ans. The Kind, the Gentle.

Q.100 What is the meaning of Al-Khabîr mentioned in 6:103?
Ans. The Aware, the Knower.

Q.101 What is the meaning of Al-Halîm mentioned in 22:59?
Ans. The Patient.

Q.102 What is the meaning of Al-Azîm mentioned in 2:255?
Ans. The Magnificent.

Q.103 What is the meaning of Al-Ghafûr mentioned in 67:2?
Ans. The Forgiver, the Much-Forgiving.

Q.104 What is the meaning of Al-Shakûr mentioned in 42:23?
Ans. The Most Grateful, Most Thankful.

Q.105 What is the meaning of Al-'Ali mentioned in 22:62?
Ans. The Most High, the Exalted.

Q.106 What is the meaning of Al-Kabîr mentioned in 31:30?
Ans. The Great, the Vast.

Q.107 What is the meaning of Al-Hafîz referred to in 11:57?
Ans. The Preserver, the Guardian, the Protector.

Q.108 What is the meaning of Al-Muqît referred to in 4:85?
Ans. The Sustainer, the Nourisher, the Provider, the Feeder, the Supporter.

Q.109 What is the meaning of Al-Hasîb referred to in 4:86?
Ans. The Generous Giver, the Accurate Judge, the Protector.

Q.110 What is the meaning of Al-Jalîl referred to in 55:27?
Ans. The Glorious, the Honourable.

Q.111 What is the meaning of Al-Karîm mentioned in 82:6?
Ans. The Generous, the Bountiful, the Kind.

Q.112 What is the meaning of Al-Raqîb mentioned in 5:117?
Ans. The Watchful, the Keeper, the Observer, the Overseer.

Q.113 What is the meaning of Al-Mujîb mentioned in 11:61?
Ans. The Answerer of Prayers, the Responsive, the Granter.

Q.114 What is the meaning of Al-Wasi mentioned in 2:247?
Ans. The Comprehensive, the All-Containing.

Q.115 What is the meaning of Al-Wadûd mentioned in 11:90?
Ans. The Loving, the Affectionate.

Q.116 What is the meaning of Al-Majîd mentioned in 85:15?
Ans. The Glorious, the Splendid, the Praiseworthy.

Q.117 What is the meaning of Al-Ba'ith referred to in 64:7?
Ans. The Resurrector, the Sender of Messengers, the Awakener of Good Qualities.

Q.118 What is the meaning of Al-Shahîd mentioned in 4:79?
Ans. The Witness, the Certifier.

Q.119 What is the meaning of Al-Haqq mentioned in 10:30?
Ans. The Truth, the Reality.

Q.120 What is the meaning of Al-Wakíl mentioned in 3:73?
Ans. The Trustee, the Guardian.

Q.121 What is the meaning of Al-Qawie mentioned in 57:25?
Ans. The Almighty.

Q.122 What is the meaning of Al-Mateen mentioned in 51:58?
Ans. The Firm, the Strong.

Q.123 What is the meaning of Al-Walî referred to in 2:107?
Ans. The Nearest Friend, the Protector, the Helper.

Q.124 What is the meaning of Al-Hamîd referred to in 35:15?
Ans. The Praiseworthy.

Q.125 What is the meaning of Al-Muhsî referred to in 36:12?
Ans. The Accountant.

Q.126 What are the meanings of Al-Mubdi and Al-Mu'îd referred to in 30:11?
Ans. The Originator, the Founder, the Beginner.
The Restorer, the Resuscitator, the Reviver.

Q.127 What are the meanings of Al-Muhyî and Al-Mumît referred to in 50:43?
Ans. The Bestower of Life.
The Causer of Death.

Q.128 What is the meaning of Al-Hayî mentioned in 40:65?
Ans. The Ever-Living, Ever-Lasting.

Q.129 What is the meaning of Al-Qayyûm mentioned in 2:255?
Ans. The Self-Existing, the Care-Taker.

Q.130 What is the meaning of Al-Wâjid referred to in 38:44?
Ans. The Finder, the Knower, the Maker.

Q.131 What is the meaning of Al-Mâjid referred to in a Hadith?
Ans. The Noble, the Glorious.

Q.132 What are the meanings of Al-Qadîr and Al-Muqtadir referred to in 23:18 and 18:45?
Ans. The Capable.
The All-Possessor of Ability.

Q.133 What are the meanings of Al-Muqaddim and Al-Mu'akhir referred to in 50:28 and 11:104?
Ans. The Promotor, the Advancer.
The Demotor, the Postponer.

Q.134 What are the meanings of Al-'Awwal and Al-Âkhir mentioned in 57:3?
Ans. The First, the Beginning and Foremost.
The Last, the End and Ultimate.

Q.135 What are the meanings of Al-Zâhir and Al-Bâtin mentioned in 57:3?
Ans. The Manifest, the Evident.
The Hidden, the Inmost Secret.

Q.136 What is the meaning of Al-Walî referred to in Hadîth?
Ans. The Governor, the Protecting Ruler.

Q.137 What is the meaning of Al-Muta'âli mentioned in 13:9?
Ans. The Most High, the Supremely Exalted.

Q.138 What is the meaning of Al-Barr mentioned in 52:28?
Ans. The Dutiful, the Kind.

Q.139 What is the meaning of Al-Tawwab mentioned in 2:128?
Ans. The Forgiver, the Acceptor or Repentance.

Q.140 What is the meaning of Al-Muntaqim referred to in 32:22?
Ans. The Punisher.

Q.141 What is the meaning of Al-'Afwu mentioned in 4:99?
Ans. The Pardoner. the Tolerant.

Q.142 What is the meaning of Al-Ra'ûf mentioned in 59:10?
Ans. The Kind, the Compassionate, the Consoling One.

Q.143 What is the meaning of Malik-Al-Mulk mentioned in 3:26?
Ans. The King of Supreme Domain.

Q.144 What is the meaning of Zu-Al-Jalâli Wal-Ikrâm mentioned in 55:27?
Ans. The Lord of Majesty and Glory and Honour.

Q.145 What is the meaning of Al-Muqsit referred to in 49:9?
Ans. The Just, the Equitable.

Q.146 What is the meaning of Al-Jamî' referred to in 6:12?
Ans. The Gatherer, the Assembler of All.

Q.147 What is the meaning of Al-Ghanî mentioned in 35:15?
Ans. The Rich, the Independent.

Q.148 What is the meaning of Al-Mughnî mentioned in 93:8?
Ans. The Enricher, the Bestower of Wealth.

Q.149 What is the meaning of Al-Mâni' mentioned in Hadith?
Ans. The Preventer, the Restrainer.

Q.150 What are the meanings of Al-Dhar and Al-Nafî referred to in 36:23?
Ans. The Distressor.
The Useful.

Q.151 What is the meaning of Al-Nûr referred to in 35:24?
Ans. The Light, the Enlightenment.

Q.152 What is the meaning fo Al-Hâdî referred to in 6:84?
Ans. The Guide.

Q.153 What is the meanig of Al-Badî mentioned in 2:117?
Ans. The Incomparable, the Originator, the Creator.

Q.154 What is the meaning of Al-Bâqî referred to in 55:27?
Ans. The Eternal, Everlasting.

Q.155 What is the meaning of Al-Wârith referred to in 15:23?
Ans. The Inheritor.

Q.156 What is the meaning of Al-Rashîd referred to in 21:51?
Ans. The Guide to the Right Path, the Unerring.

Q.157 What is the meaning of Al-Sabûr referred to in 16:121?
Ans. The Most Patient.

CHAPTER 5

AL-IBADAT

Q. 1 What is the second principle of Islam?

Ans. To offer the five obligatory prayers (Salah) daily.

Q.2 What is Wudu'?

Ans. The act of washing the hands, the mouth, the nose, the face, the arms, the hair, the ears and the feet before praying.

Q.3 What are the two prerequisites to perform Wudu'?

Ans. To make sure that the water is clean and to have the intention of performing the Wudu' for offering prayers.

Q.4 Can you name the parts of the body you wash during Wudu' and how many times you wash them?

Ans. Hands up to the wrists (3 times), mouth and gargle with water (3 times), face (3 times), right, then left arm up to the elbow (3 times), hair (1 time), ears (1 time), right then left foot up to the ankles and between the toes (3 times).

Q.5 What is Ghusl?

Ans. Washing all parts of the body including the hair at least once a week and after sexual intercourse, discharge of semen (for men) or completion of menses and confinement (for women).

Q.6 How do you perform Ghusl?

Ans. After having the intention of performing Ghusl, the hands are washed up to the wrists three times, then the private parts are washed thoroughly three times, the whole body is cleaned, the Wudu' is performed and finally all parts of the body are washed thoroughly, including the hair.

Q.7 Can you name three acts that make Wudu' void?

Ans. Passage of matter, including wind from the private parts and loss of consciousness through sleep or drowsiness.

Q. 8 Does Wudu' convey any other meaning besides the cleanliness of the body?

Ans. Yes, spiritual cleanliness and purity.

Q. 9 What is Tayammum?

Ans. The act of cleaning parts of the body, replacing Wudu' if one does not find or cannot use water.

Q.10 How do you perform Tayammum?

Ans. To strike pure earth lightly with palms of both hands, pass the hands over the face once then again strike lightly pure earth with the palms and rub alternately the arms and the hands.

Q.11 Is Tayammum nullified with the same reasons as Wudu'?

Ans. Yes, in addition Tayammum is nulified if the cause of performing it is not there. For example, if water becomes accessible.

Q.12 Can you use the sea water to perform Wudu'?

Ans. Yes.

Q.13 Can you use the rain water to perform Wudu'?

Ans. Yes.

Q.14 True or False: When you do Wudu' you have to use water economically, even if it is from the sea.

Ans. True.

Q.15 True or False: It is recommended to have Wudu' before you touch the Qur'ân.

Ans. True.

Q.16 True or False: It is recommended that you make Wudu' before you go to bed.

Ans. True.

Q.17 True or False: You must perform Wudu' before every Salah.

Ans. False.

Q.18 True or False: Ghusl should be performed on the body of a dead Muslim.

Ans. True.

Q.19 True or False: It is highly recommended that Ghusl is performed on Fridays and the days of the two Fastivals (Eid).

Ans. True.

Q.20 What is Azan?

Ans. First call to announce that it is time to offer the obligatory prayer.

Q.21 How is Azan recited?

Ans. Allâh (God) is most great (*Allâhu Akbar*), four times

I bear witness that there is no god but God (*Ash-hadu An-lâ-ilâha Illallâh*), twice

I bear witness that Muhammad (ﷺ) is the messenger of God (*Ash-hadu Anna Muhammadar-Rasûl-Allâh*), twice.

Come to prayer (*Hayya alas-Salah*), twice

Come to success (*Hayya alal-Falah*), twice

God is most great (*Allâhu Akbar*), twice

There is no god but Allâh (*Lâ ilâha Illallâh*), once.

Q.22 What is the extra phrase which is used in the Azan of the early morning prayer (Fajr)?

Ans. After "Come to success" you say "Prayer is better than sleep (*As salâtu Khairun Minan-naum*)", twice.

Q.23 What is Iqamah?

Ans. The second call to prayer and is recited immediately before the beginning of the obligatory prayer.

Q.24 How is Iqamah recited?

Ans. One way to do it is the same as Azan, except add after "Come to success", "Prayer has indeed begun (Qad qamat-is-salah)", twice.

Q.25 Can you name the five daily obligatory (Fard) prayers and their times?

Ans. Early morning prayer (Fajr), after dawn and before sunrise, Noon prayer (Zuhr), after the sun begins to decline and last until it is midway to setting, Afternoon prayer ('Asr), after the sun is midway to setting until it begins to set, Evening prayer

(Maghrib), after the sun sets and before the disappearance of the day light, and Night prayer ('Isha), after the disappearance of the daylight and before dawn, but preferably before midnight.

Q.26 What is a Rak'a?

Ans. A unit of prayer.

Q.27 How many Rak'a are each obligatory prayer?

Ans. Fajr (two), Zuhr (four), Asr (four), Maghrib (three), and Isha (four).

Q.28 Can you describe one complete Rak'a?

Ans. Standing erect (Qiyam) and placing the right hand upon the left, below or above the navel, recite some verses from the Qur'ân, bowing down (Ruku') keeping the back straight, qiyam again, prostrating down (Sujûd) with both palms (not elbows), forehead, nose, knees and toes of both feet touching the ground, sitting down in a reverential position (Qu'ûd) keeping the right foot erect on the toes and the left one in a reclining position and another (Sujûd).

Q.29 What do you say to begin your prayer?

Ans. God is most great (Allâhu Akbar).

Q.30 What verses of the Qur'ân do you recite during the Qiyam of each Rak'a?

Ans. For the first and second you recite the opening chapter (Sûrah) of the Qur'ân (Al Fatiha) and some other verses and for any Rak'a after the second you recite only Al-Fatiha.

Q.31 What do you recite during each Ruku' of each Rak'a?

Ans. Glory to my Lord, the Great (*Subhana Rabbiyal-Azîm*), three times.

Q.32 What do you recite during each Sujûd of each Rak'a?

Ans. Glory to my Lord, the Most High (*Subhâna Rabbiyal 'Ala*), three times.

Q.33 What do you recite when you finish Ruku' and while standing erect again?

Ans. God has listened to the one who has praised Him (*Sami' Allâhu liman Hamidah*), our Lord praise to You (*Rabbana Laka Al-Hamd*), once.

Q.34 How does the first Rak'a end?

Ans. It ends up in a Sujûd.

Q.35 How does the second Rak'a end?

Ans. It ends up in Qu'ud and reciting the first half of Tasha-hud if this Rak'a is not the last Rak'a and all of the Tasha-hud if it is the last Rak'a.

Q.36 How does the third Rak'a end?

Ans. It ends up in Qu'ud and reciting all of Tasha-hud if it is the last Rak'a, or it ends up in Sujûd if it is not the last Rak'a.

Q.37 How does the fourth (and last) Rak'a end?

Ans. It ends up in Qu'ud and reciting all of the Tasha-hud.

Q.38 Which direction do you face when you pray?

Ans. The direction of the Ka'ba in Makka.

Q.39 Can you name four things that nullify a prayer?

Ans. Talking, any act that nullifies Wudu', turning away from the Ka'ba, exposing parts of the body (between the navel and the knees, in the case of males and any part of the body except the hands and the face in the case of the females).

Q.40 When should one shorten the five obligatory prayers?

Ans. When one is travelling. In this case the four Rak'a prayers become two.

Q.41 What is the Friday Congregational Prayer (Salat-Al-Juma)?

Ans. A congregational prayer which is offered on the afternoon of Fridays. It is of two Rak'a and is proceeded by a Khutba given by an Imam (prayer leader). It replaces Zuhr prayer.

Q.42 Who should be chosen to lead any prayers?

Ans. One among those present who is conversant in the Qur'ân.

Q.43 What other prayers highly recommended to be offered in congregations?

Ans. The five obligatory daily prayers.

Q.44 How many Rak'a do the feasts' prayers (Id-ul-Fitr and Id-ul-Adha) have?

Ans. Two each and must be offered in congregations.

Q.45 Are there any Khutba associated with the two feasts' (Eid) prayers?

Ans. Yes, and they are given after the prayer.

Q.46 In which Rak'a is the recitation of the Qur'ân made audible?

Ans. The two Rak'a of Fajr, the first two Rak'a of Maghrib and 'Isha, the two Rak'a of Juma prayer, the two Rak'a of both Eid prayers and in all the Rak'a of the Taraweeh prayers (those performed after 'Isha during the month of Ramadan).

Q.47 Is Salah obligatory even during sickness or during travelling?

Ans. Yes.

Q.48 Who is exempted from Salah for a certain period?

Ans. A sleeping person until he wakes up, a child until he/she becomes an adult, a woman during her menses or confinement after child birth, and a mad person until he/she recovers.

Q.49 What are the times in which any Salah should not be offered?

Ans. Just before and during sunrise and just before and during sunset.

Q.50 What should the listener do during the Azan?

Ans. He/she should repeat each part, except when he/she listens to (*Hayya-alas-Salah*) and (*Hayya alal-Falah*) should say (*La Hawla Wala Quwwata Illa Billah*); God is the only source of Power and Might, and when he/she listens to (*As Salatu Khairum Minannaum*) should say (Sadaqat); you have told the truth.

Q.51 True or False: When travelling in a moving vehicle or when confined to a hospital bed you can perform Salah without facing the Ka'ba.

Ans. True.

Q.52 What do you say after Al-Fatiha in each Rak'a?

Ans. Âmîn, meaning Oh Allâh, please accept.

Q.53 True or False: It is highly recommended that you say Âmîn loudly if the Imam saying it loudly.

Ans. True.

Q.54 In which Rak'a do you recite audibly from the Qur'ân if you pray alone?

Ans. In the first two Rak'a of Fajr and the first two Rak'a of Maghrib and 'Isha.

Q.55 Do you have to recite out loud the Qur'ân along with the Imam as he recites it out loud?

Ans. No, you should listen and follow his recitation.

Q.56 What is the Sunnah Mu'akada (highly recommended) prayer for Fajr?

Ans. Two Rak'a before the obligatory (Fard) prayer.

Q.57 What is the Sunnah Mu'akada Prayer for Zuhr?

Ans. Two (or four), before and four (or two) Rak'a after.

Q.58 What is the Sunnah Mu'akada prayer for Maghrib?

Ans. Two Rak'a after.

Q.59 What is the Sunnah Mu'akada prayer for 'Isha?

Ans. Two Rak'a after.

Q.60 What is the Sunnah Ghair-Mu'akada (just recommended) prayer for 'Asr?

Ans. Two or four Rak'a before the obligatory (Fard) prayer.

Q.61 What is the Sunnah Ghair-Mu'akada prayer for Maghrib?

Ans. Two Rak'a before.

Q.62 What is the Sunnah Ghair-Mu'akada prayer for 'Isha?

Ans. Two Rak'a before.

Q.63 What is the Witr prayer?

Ans. To pray an odd number of Rak'a (one, three, five, ...etc.) after 'Isha after its Sunnah prayer.

Q.64 Is the Witr a Sunnah Mu'akada (highly recommended) prayer?

Ans. Yes.

Q.65 What is Qunoot?

Ans. A special Du'a asking Allâh special request especially in the time of distress, done after saying "*Sami Allâhu liman Hamidah*" in the last Rak'at of the five Fard prayers and Witr prayer.

Q.66 What is Qayam-Al-Layel?

Ans. To be up during part of or all of the night performing Salah after 'Isha and it's best time is the last third of the night.

Q.67 How many Rak'a do you in Qayam-Al-Layel?

Ans. Any even number followed by a Witr prayer (if you have not done it).

Q.68 What is Quam Ramadan (Salat-Al-Tarawih)?

Ans. To pray in Ramadan, after 'Isha and before the Witr prayer, eight Rak'at (two at a time) preferable in a congregation at the Mosque. You can do more than eight but even number.

Q.69 What is Salat-Al-Duha?

Ans. To pray an even number of Rak'at, between 10 mins after sunrise and noon.

Q.70 Is praying in a congregation (Jam'a) highly recommended for Fard prayers?

Ans. Yes, its reward is many fold compared to praying alone.

Q.71 How many people are needed for Jam'a?

Ans. Two or more.

Q.72 Can women go to Mosques to pray Jam'a?

Ans. Yes.

Q.73 True or False: The Imam in Jam'a should recite a long Sûrah?

Ans. False, he should recite short Sûrah because the group could have the unfit, the unwell and children.

Q.74 Can a woman Imam lead Jam'a of women?

Ans. Yes.

Q.75 If Jam'a prayer is in progress can you join it?

Ans. Yes, and complete the missing Rak'at.

Q.76 In Jama, where do people stand to pray relative to the Imam?

Ans. If one, stands to his right, if more, stand behind him in rows; the men, then the children, then the women.

Q.77 What is Ta'hia Al-Masjid?

Ans. A prayer of two Rak'at performed after you enter the Mosque and before sitting.

Q.78 Can you talk in the Mosque at times other than the time of prayers?

Ans. Yes, with allowable topics.

Q.79 Can you eat, drink and sleep in the Mosque?

Ans. Yes, but keeping the place clean.

Q.80 True or False: People are not allowed to cross in front of a person praying for a distance of an arm length.

Ans. True.

Q.81 True or False: A Non-Muslim is allowed to enter the Mosque.

Ans. True.

Q.82 Can a person in prayer move if necessary?

Ans. Yes, as long as he/she still faces the Ka'ba.

Q.83 Can a person in prayer carry a child if necessary?

Ans. Yes.

Q.84 Can a person hold and read from the text of Qur'ân during his/her prayer?

Ans. Yes, in non-obligatory prayers.

Q.85 True or False: A person should not look towards the sky while praying but down towards the front.

Ans. True.

Q.86 True or False: A person can open or close his/her eyes while praying.

Ans. True.

Q.87 True or False: If prayer time and a meal time are close, the person should eat first.

Ans. True.

Q.88 True or False: Laughing during the prayer will invalidate the prayer.

Ans. True.

Q.89 True or False: If a prayer is not performed on time, it should be performed as soon as possible afterwards.

Ans. True.

Q.90 What is the general rule to perform Salah during travel?

Ans. To shorten the four Rak'at prayers to two and to combine Zuhr and 'Asr at either time and to combine Maghrib and 'Isha at either time.

Q.91 True of False: A Muslim should try to avoid travelling on Friday; not to miss Friday prayer.

Ans. True.

Q.92 True of False: Every Muslim, male or female, young or old, should have his/her best clothes cleaned and perfumed for Islamic gatherings, eg Friday congregational prayer and Eid prayers.

Ans. True.

Q.93 True or False: If Eid Prayer is on a Friday, the Friday prayer is not obligatory on that day.

Ans. True.

Q.94 True or False: A Muslim should eat before going out for Eid-Al-Fitr prayer and should eat after coming back from Eid-Al-Adha prayer.

Ans. True.

Q.95 True or False: For Eid prayers, there is no Azan or Eqama.

Ans. True.

Q.96 True or False: For Eid prayers, the Khutba is after the prayers.

Ans. True.

Q.97 What is Zakah (Islamic Alms-Tax)?

Ans. The amount of money (or in kind) which a Muslim must give to the deserving every year.

Q.98 What is the annual rate of Zakah on the money in your possession?

Ans. A minimum of 2.5% of the value of the accumulated wealth above basic needs which have been in one's possession for 12 lunar months.

Q.99 Among what groups of Muslims is Zakah to be distributed?

Ans. The poor and the needy, the salary of collectors of Zakah, the new converts, freeing Muslim slaves and Muslim prisoners of war, Muslims in debt, cost of defence and propagation of Islam, building schools, hospitals, etc., and Muslim wayfarers.

Q.100 What moral does Zakah convey to you?

Ans. Not to be selfish and to be willing to share Allâh's provisions with others.

Q.101 What is Zakah-Al-Fitr?

Ans. A Sunnah Mu'akada (highly recommended) annual charity given in the last days of Ramadan or on the day of Eid-Al-Fitr.

Q.102 What is the amount of Zakah-Al-Fitr?

Ans. About $7.00 (in 1987) for every Muslim and his dependants including children.

Q.103 To whom should Zakah-Al-Fitr be given?

Ans. To those who merit Zakah.

Q.104 True or False: Zakah is due on any extra accumulation of wealth, above basic need, (Nesab) valued at $30.00 (in 1987) or more which was in the possession of a Muslim for one lunar year (Hawel).

Ans. True

Q.105 True or False: A Muslim who is responsible for the financial management of the wealth of children and the infirm should pay Zakah on their behalf from their money.

Ans. True.

Q.106 True or False: When a Muslim dies before paying Zakah it should be paid before distributing his/her estate.
Ans. True.

Q.107 True or False: Zakah must be paid on extra accumulation of wealth (Nesab) only after it is in the possession of a Muslim for one lunar year (Hawel).
Ans. False. Zakah can be paid even if the lunar year is not over.

Q.108 True or False: Zakah is an act of Islamic worship and should be given to Muslims.
Ans. True.

Q.109 True or False: Needy non-Muslims should get help from Muslims through Sadaqa; the charity given extra to the Zakah.
Ans. True.

Q.110 True or False: Zakah should not be given to the Muslim's needy offspring (children, grandchildren, etc.), the Muslim's needy parents, grandparents, or his needy wife.
Ans. True. Their support is mandatory, a duty and a resonsibility which comes before Zakah.

Q.111 True or False: Zakah can be given from a rich wife to her needy husband.
Ans. True because his support is not her duty and responsibility.

Q.112 True or False: Zakah should be spent on the Muslims who deserve it in the same city and if there is extra, it should be sent to further places.
Ans. True.

Q.113 True or False: Zakah Al-Fitr can be given to a non-Muslim.
Ans. True.

Q.114 True or False; Any charity giving more than Zakah is called Sadaqa.
Ans. True.

Q.115 True or False: Sadaqa is given to the close needy persons; children, wife, parents, husband, relatives, first before giving to others.
Ans. True.

Q.116 True or False: Sadaqa is given in money or in kind, even a smile is a Sadaqa.
Ans. True.

Q.117 What does fasting (Seyam) mean in Islam?
Ans. Abstaining from eating, drinking, smoking, allowing anything to enter into the body and sexual intercourse, from the break of dawn until the sunset.

Q.118 When is fasting obligatory (Fard)?
Ans. During the month of Ramadan.

Q.119 On whom is the fast of Ramadan obligatory?
Ans. All Muslim adults, except the insane and the invalid.

Q.120 Who is exempted from observing the obligatory fast?
Ans. Men and women too old or too sick or their work is too hazardous to bear the hardship of a fast, but they have to feed a needy Muslim daily during the month of Ramadan or donate the equivalent.

Q.121 Under what circumstances can one defer (or must defer) Can defer
Ans. (a) If one is sick
(b) If a woman is nursing a child
(c) If a person is traveller
(d) If a woman is pregnant

Must defer: a woman during her period of menstruation.

Q.122 What moral does fasting convey to you?
Ans. Self-control and it makes the practice of virtue easier.

Q.123 What are the main Sunnah for observing a fast?
Ans. (a) taking a meal (called Sohoor) before the break of dawn
(b) eating dates and drinking water after sunset at the time of breaking the fast, before eating the main meal,
(c) reciting the following Du'a prior to breaking the fast: "Oh God, for Thy sake I have fasted and now I break the fast on what You have provided."

Q.124 What is the penalty for not fasting for a valid reason in Ramadan?

Ans. 1. To observe the days of fasting after Ramadan and repenting (if breaking the fast during Ramadan was by eating or drinking).

2. To observe sixty days of fasting or feeding sixty persons in place of one day of Ramadan (if breaking the fast during Ramadan was by sexual contacts with wife/husband).

Q.125 Is the fast made void if one breaks the fast by mistake?

Ans. No.

Q.126 True or False: A Muslim should not voluntarily fast the two days of Eid (that of Eid-ul-Fitr and Eid-ul-Adha).

Ans. True.

Q.127 True or False: A Muslim should not voluntarily fast a Friday or a Saturday by itself.

Ans. True.

Q.128 True or False: A Muslims should not voluntarily fast the three days after Eid-ul-Adha.

Ans. True.

Q.129 True or False: It is Sunnah to voluntarily fast six days after Eid-ul-Fitr, during the month of Shawal.

Ans. True.

Q.130 True or False: A Muslim should voluntarily fast year round if he/she can.

Ans. False. Fasting year round is prohibited. The maximum is fasting alternative days.

Q.131 True or False: It is Sunnah to voluntarily fast the day of 'Arafa if you are not performing Hajj (the day immediately before Eid-ul-Adha, when every Haji is at Mount Arafat).

Ans. True.

Q.132 True or False: It is Sunnah to voluntarily fast Mondays and Thursdays.

Ans. True.

Q.133 True or False: It is Sunnah to voluntarily fast the 9th and 10th days of Moharram (the first month of the Islamic calendar).

Ans. True.

Q.134 True or False: It is Sunnah to voluntarily fast the 13th, 14th, and 15th days of each Islamic month.

Ans. True.

Q.135 True or False: When you voluntarily fast a day, you are not allowed to break the fast.

Ans. False.

Q.136 True or False: When fasting, you should break the fast immediately after sunset.

Ans. True.

Q.137 True or False: If you are cooking and you taste the food, you have not broken your fast.

Ans. True, as long you did not swallow.

Q.138 True or False: If you intend to break your fast during the day, your fast is not valid, even if you did not eat or drink.

Ans. True.

Q.139 True or False: If a Muslim dies before he/she made up a missed fasting days of Ramadan, one of his relatives can do it on his/her behalf.

Ans. True.

Q.140 What is the name of the important night which occurs during one of the last ten nights of the month of Ramadan?

Ans. Laila-tul-Qadr, the night of might and power.

Q.141 When is Laila-tul-Qadr?

Ans. On one of the odd nights of the last ten days of Ramadan; the night of the 21, 23, 25, 27, 29. Most likely the night of the 27th.

Q.142 What is E'tikaf?

Ans. Staying in the Mosque for a period of time for Salah and studying Qur'ân, any time but especially during the last 10 days of Ramadan.

Q.143 True or False: E'tikaf must be at night.

Ans. False, it could be at any time, day or night.

Q.144 True or False: While in E'tikaf, a Muslim must fast.

Ans. False, he/she could fast or not.

Q.145 On whom is the performance of Hajj (pilgrimage to Mekka) obligatory?

Ans. On the adult Muslim, male or female, who is physically fit and who can afford the trip to Mecca.

Q.146 What is Hajj?

Ans. The pilgrimage to Mecca in the state of Ihram and observing Wuqûf (being present) at Arafat and other prescribed actions in the first 10 days in the month of Zul-Hija (the 12th lunar month).

Q.147 What does Ihram mean for men?

Ans. The intention of performing Hajj and/or Umra and the removal of all clothes and wrapping the body in a couple of seamless sheets after making Ghusl and Wudu' and Shaving the hair off the private parts and under the arms and wearing simple footwear which does not cover the ankles and having the intention (Niyyat) to perform Hajj.

Q.148 What is the difference between the adoption of Ihram by men and women?

Ans. The women wear sewn clothes and cover the head but not the face and they are allowed to wear socks. The rest of the requirements are the same as for men.

Q.149 What is Tawaf?

Ans. Walking around the Ka'ba seven times commencing from the black stone and having the Ka'ba on one's left.

Q.150 What is Sa'ie?

Ans. Marching between the two hills of Safa and Marwa, near the Ka'ba, seven times.

Q.151 What is Wuqoof?

Ans. Being present by the plains of Arafat (7 miles from Mekka) at least for a few moments during the time between the declining of the sun on the 9th day of Zul-Hijja and the dawn of the 10th day.

Q.152 What are the Miqat?

Ans. They are of two types; geographical; the boundary lines outside Mekka at which the pilgrims have to be in the state of Ihram and of specific dates; the months of Shawal, Zul-Qa'da and Zul-Hijja.

Q.153 How do you perform Hajj?

Ans.
1. Be in the state of Ihram before the Miqate.
2. Perform the first Tawaf (called Tawaf-Al-Qudûm)
3. On the 8th day fo Zul-Hijja go to Mina (a town 3 miles from Mekka) before Zuhr prayer and stay one night.
4. On the 9th day after Fajr prayer proceeds to Arafat and stay in any area surrounding the Hill of Mercy (Jabl-Rahmat).
5. Just after sunset leave Arafat to Muzdalifa (a place between Mina and Arafat), perform both Maghrib and 'Isha prayers, where the 'Isha prayer is shortened to two Rak'at and pick up at least 49 pebbles (small stones).
6. Stay in Muzdalifa overnight and leave after the Fajr prayer (10th day) to Mina.
7. On the 10th day of Zul-Hijja throw 7 of the pebbles at a pillar called (Jâmrat-Al-Aqubah) and then make a sacrifice of a goat or a sheep or a camel to eat and to distribute to the poor.
8. After finishing step 7, men shave part of their head or the whole head and women cut of at least an inch of their hair. At that time the state of Ihram is partially over.
9. Following step 8, proceed to Mekka to perform a second Tawaf (called Tawaf-Al-Ifada) and a second Sa'ie.
10. Return to Mina and spend the night.

11. On the 11th and 12th days, throw 7 of the pebbles on each of the three pillars. If the pilgrim stays until the 13th day as well, he or she throws pebbles as they did on the 11th and 12th days.

12. Return to Mekka and perform the last departing Tawaf before leaving to your country (called Tawaf-Al-Wida).

Q.154 What is Umra?

Ans. The visit to Makka at any time of the year in the state of Ihram and perform Tawaf and Sa'ie.

Q.155 What things become unlawful in the state of Ihram?

Ans. Hunting, sexual intercourse or its preliminaries, shaving of hair, cutting nails, using any perfume and killing any animal or insect unless one's life is in danger.

Q.156 Is visiting the Prophet's Mosque in Madina part of performing Hajj?

Ans. No, but it is highly recommended after (or before) performing Hajj to pay a visit to the Prophet's Mosque.

Q.157 Can Hajj and Umra be performed in the same state of Ihram?

Ans. Yes, this is called Qiran.

Q.158 What is Tamattu?

Ans. It is when Umra is performed in the month of Shawal, Zul-Al-Qa'da or Zul-Al-Hijja, Ihram state is terminated and then reinstated again on the 7th of Zul-Hijja at Makka to perform Hajj.

Q.159 What is Ifrad?

Ans. If one performs Hajj alone and not Umra.

CHAPTER 6

THE STORIES OF PROPHETS IN THE QUR'ÂN

Q. 1 How many Prophets of Allâh have been mentioned by name in the Qur'ân?

Ans. 25.

Q.2 Who are Prophets mentioned in the Qur'ân?

Ans. Adam (A.S.) (Adam) Idrîs (A.S.) (Enoch), Nûh (A.S.) (Noah), Hûd (A.S.), Saleh (A.S.) (Salih), Ibrâhim (A.S.) (Abraham), Ismâ'îl (A.S.) (Ishmael), Ishaq (A.S.) (Isac), Loot (A.S.) (Lot), Ya'qub (A.S.) (Jacob), Yusuf (A.S.) (Joseph), Shu'aib (A.S.), Ayyub (A.S.) (Job), Mûsâ (A.S.) (Moses), Harûn (A.S.) (Aaron), Zul-Kafil (A.S.) (Ezekiel), Dawûd (A.S.) (David), Sulaimân (A.S.) (Soloman) Ilias (A.S.) (Elias), Al-Yasa' (A.S.) (Elisha), Yunus (A.S.) (Jonah), Zakaria (A.S.) (Zacharius), Yahya (A.S.) (John), 'Isa (A.S.) (Jesus) and Muhammad (ﷺ), peace be upon them all.

Q.3 Who created Adam (A.S.)?

Ans. Allâh, the Almighty.

Q.4 From what did Allâh create Adam (A.S.)?

Ans. From clay.

Q.5 What did Allâh order the Angels to do after He created Adam (A.S.)?

Ans. To bow down to show their reverence to him.

Q.6 Did all the Angels obey Allâh's order?

Ans. Yes.

Q.7 Who did not obey Allâh's order to bow to Adam (A.S.)?

Ans. Iblîs (Satan) refused. He said I am better than Adam (A.S.) because I am created from fire while Adam is created from clay.

Q.8 Who did Allâh create from his very nature as Adam (A.S.)?

Ans. Adam's (A.S.) wife.

Q.9 What did Allâh order Adam (A.S.) and his wife to do?

Ans. To live in Paradise and enjoy its good things but not to approach a certain tree.

Q.10 Did Adam (A.S.) and his wife obey Allâh's order?

Ans. Yes, but Satan whispered evil to them until they ate from the forbidden tree.

Q.11 What happened after Adam (A.S.) and his wife ate from the tree?

Ans. Allâh ordered Adam (A.S.) and his wife to get out of Paradise. Adam (A.S.) repented of his sin and that of his wife and Allâh forgave them and gave them guidance.

Q.12 What did the people of Nûh (A.S.) worship?

Ans. Idols.

Q.13 What did Allâh do to guide the people of Nûh (A.S.)?

Ans. Allâh sent Nûh (A.S.) to his people to call them to worship Allâh alone and warn them of severe punishment if they did not.

Q.14 Did the people of Nûh (A.S.) follow him to worship Allâh alone?

Ans. No, except for very few.

Q.15 What did Nûh (A.S.) ask Allâh when most of his people did not believe in worshipping Allâh alone?

Ans. Nûh (A.S.) asked Allâh "O my Lord, Do not leave of the unbelievers a single one on earth".

Q.16 What did Allâh order Nûh (A.S.) to do?

Ans. To construct an Ark and to place in it two of each kind of bird and animal; a male and female and also his family except for his wife, because she did not believe. The believers joined him.

Q.17 What happened after Nûh (A.S.) built the Ark?

Ans. With commands from Allâh, the earth experienced a huge flood and the sky sent a heavy rain. The waves were as high as mountains.

Q.18 Did Nûh's (A.S.) son join him in the Ark?

Ans. No. Nûh (A.S.) called him to believe in Allâh and to join him. He disobeyed and he said that he would be saved by going on top of a mountain. But the waves overwhelmed Nûh's (A.S.) son.

Q.19 To whom was Prophet Hûd (A.S.) sent?

Ans. To 'Âd (A.S.), an ancient people living in land between Arabia and Yemen.

Q.20 What did Prophet Hûd (A.S.) ask his people to worship?

Ans. Allâh alone.

Q.21 What happened to the people of 'Âd (A.S.), after they disobeyed Prophet Hûd (A.S.)?

Ans. They were destroyed by a fierce wind which Allâh caused to blow against them for seven nights and eight days.

Q.22 To whom was Prophet Saleh (A.S.) sent?

Ans. To Thamûd (A.S.), an ancient people living in a land between Arabia and Syria.

Q.23 What did Allâh give Prophet Saleh (A.S.) as a sign of Prophecy?

Ans. A she-camel which knew that it had a right of using a watering source at a certain time and on other times the right was for people.

Q.24 What did Thamûd (A.S.) do to Prophet Saleh's (A.S.) she-camel?

Ans. They slaughtered her.

Q.25 How did Allâh punish Thamûd (A.S.), after they disobeyed their Prophet Saleh (A.S.)?

Ans. They were destroyed by a dreadful earthquake.

Q.26 To whom was Prophet Shu'aib (A.S.) sent?

Ans. To the people of Madyan who lived between the Sinai Peninsula and Palestine.

Q.27 What did Prophet Shu'aib (A.S.) tell his people?

Ans. To worship Allâh alone and to stop giving short measure or weight to the goods they sold.

Q.28 What did Prophet Shu'aib (A.S.) warn his people?

Ans. He warned them of a fate similar to that of the people of Nûh (A.S.) or Hûd (A.S.) or Saleh (A.S.), if they did not worship Allâh and follow his commandments.

Q.29 How did the people of Madyan respond to Prophet Shu'aib (A.S.)?

Ans. They made mockery of him and threatened that they would drive him and the few believers out of Madyan.

Q.30 How did Allâh punish the people of Madyan?

Ans. They were destroyed with an earthquake except for Prophet Shu'aib (A.S.) and the believers.

Q.31 Where did Prophet Shu'aib (A.S.) go after the destruction of Madyan?

Ans. To a group of people near Madyan, called "Ashâb-al-Ayka" or the people of the wood, so called because they used a lot of wood in their building.

Q.32. How did Allâh punish "the people of the wood"?

Ans. Allâh sent them very severe heat for seven days continuously and when they gathered to take shelter under a big cloud, Allâh caused fire to rain upon them.

Q.33 How did Prophet Ibrahim (A.S.) show his people that the idols they were worshipping did not understand?

Ans. He broke the idols and said that the biggest idol is the one who did it and they should ask him about the full story.

Q.34 How did the people of Prophet Ibrahim (A.S.) respond to him?

Ans. They ordered him to be burned, but Allâh caused the fire to be cool and he was saved.

Q.35 What did Prophet Ibrahim (A.S.) ask Allâh for, when he was old?

Ans. "O my Lord, grant me a righteous son".

Q.36 Who are the sons of Prophet Ibrahim (A.S.)?

Ans. Ismail (A.S.) and Ishaq (A.S.).

Q.37 What is the famous story which happened to Prophet Ibrahim (A.S.) and his son Ismail (A.S.)?

Ans. Prophet Ibrahim (A.S.) said to Prophet Ismail (A.S.) "I saw in a vision that I must offer you in a sacrifice.". His son replied "Do as you are commanded. As his son was ready to be sacrificed, Prophet Ibrahim (A.S.) was inspired by Allâh that he had already fulfilled his vision. Allâh put a lamb in place of Ismail (A.S.).

Q.38 How do Muslims commemorate the famous story of Prophets Ibrahim (A.S.) and Ismail (A.S.)?

Ans. By sacrificing a ram or a sheep every year in Eid-ul-Adhah, which occurs in the season of Hajj (pilgrimage).

Q.39 Who are the father and grandfather of Prophet Yusuf (A.S.)?

Ans. Prophet Ya'qub (A.S.) and Prophet Ishaq (A.S.).

Q.40 How many other sons did Prophet Ya'qub (A.S.) have in addition to Prophet Yusuf (A.S.)?

Ans. Eleven.

Q.41 What is the story of Prophet Yusuf (A.S.) with his brothers?

Ans. When Yusuf's (A.S.) brothers noticed that he was the best-loved son by their father, they were filled with envy and hate. They plotted to get rid of him and threw him down into a well. Some merchants found him and sold him to an Egyptian with great wealth and power.

Q.42 Why was Prophet Yusuf (A.S.) imprisoned in Egypt?

Ans. Because of a scandal raised by the wife of his Egyptian master.

Q.43 What did Prophet Yusuf (A.S.) do in prison?

Ans. He taught his fellow prisoners the message of Truth and he was known for Allâh's gift of interpreting dreams.

Q.44 Who released Prophet Yusuf (A.S.) from prison and why?

Ans. The King of Egypt, after Prophet Yusuf (A.S.) interpreted a dream by the King.

Q.45 How did the King of Egypt reward Prophet Yusuf (A.S.)?

Ans. He made him a minister.

Q.46 What happened to Prophet Yusuf's (A.S.) brothers after he became a minister in Egypt?

Ans. Driven by famine, they came to Egypt to search for food. Yusuf (A.S.) treated them well, without their knowing him and asked them to bring their youngest brother next time.

Q.47 How did Prophet Yusuf's (A.S.) father Prophet Ya'qub (A.S.) come to Egypt?

Ans. Prophet Yusuf (A.S.) detained his youngest brother and asked his brothers to bring their father Prophet Ya'qub (A.S.) and the whole family from Palestine to Egypt.

Q.48 What is the other name of Prophet Ya'qub (A.S.)?

Ans. Isra'îl.

Q.49 Who did the offspring (children) of Prophet Isra'îl "Ya'qub (A.S.)" worship in Egypt?

Ans. They were not idolatrous like the people of Egypt at that time, and they worshipped Allâh alone.

Q.50 How did the King of Egypt treat the children of Isra'îl?

Ans. For four centuries the children of Isra'îl were treated well but later the Pharoahs treated them badly and used to slaughter every male child born to them.

Q.51 Why did the Pharoahs treat the children of Isra'îl this way?

Ans. First, because they were worshipping one God and not idols or the Pharoah himself, and because they were foreigners and did not mingle with the Egyptians.

Q.52 How was Allâh gracious to the children of Isra'îl?

Ans. Allâh delivered them the Pharoah with Prophet Mûsâ (A.S.).

Q.53 Who was the father, great grandfather, and brother of Prophet Mûsâ (A.S.)?

Ans. Imran, Ya'qub and Harûn (A.S.).

Q.54 How was Prophet Mûsâ (A.S.) saved from being slaughtered by the Pharoahs when he was a baby?

Ans. When he was born, his mother had a revelation that she should cast him into the river. After she died, he was picked up by the Pharoah's people and the Pharoah's wife ordered him not to be slain as she had no boys.

Q.55 How did Prophet Musa's (A.S.) mother get to see him after he went to the Pharaoh's palaces?

Ans. After his mother cast him in the river, she ordered his sister to watch him to learn who would pick him up. Allâh ordained the child Mûsâ (A.S.) to refuse to suckle any woman's milk, so his sister told the Pharoah's people that she knew of a woman that would nourish him and bring him up, and that woman was actually his mother.

Q.56 Did the child Mûsâ (A.S.) return back to the Pharoah's palace?

Ans. Yes, and he was brought up in the royal family, with the best of facilities and teachers.

Q.57 How did Prophet Mûsâ (A.S.) kill an Egyptian?

Ans. One day he found an Israelite being oppressed by an Egyptian so he struck the Egyptian by his fist. The Egyptian was accidentally killed and Mûsâ (A.S.) fled Egypt to Madyan near Palestine.

Q.58 How did Mûsâ (A.S.) get married in Madyan?

Ans. Mûsâ (A.S.) helped two sisters to water their flocks from a well. Their father rewarded him by allowing him to marry one in return for Mûsâ (A.S.) serving him for eight years. Mûsâ (A.S.) accepted and fulfilled the term.

Q.59 How did Allâh order Prophet Mûsâ (A.S.) to go back to Egypt?

Ans. While Prophet Mûsâ (A.S.) was journeying with his wife, he perceived a fire in the direction of a mountain. He left his family and went to the direction of the fire to bring some burning boards for his family. He heard a voice say "O Mûsâ (A.S.)! Verily I am Allâh the Lord of the worlds." Allâh ordered Prophet Mûsâ (A.S.) to go to the Pharoah and his people to call them to worship Allâh alone.

Q.60 What did Prophet Mûsâ (A.S.) say after Allâh commanded him to go the Pharoah?

Ans. "My Lord, I killed a person among them and I fear that they will kill me and my brother Harûn (A.S.) is more eloquent in speech than I. Send him with me as a helper."

Q.61 What did Prophet Mûsâ (A.S.) say to the Pharaoh?

Ans. "Truly, I am a messenger from the Lord of the Worlds" and asked him to let the people of Israel go with him.

Q.62 How did the Pharaoh respond to Prophet Mûsâ (A.S.)?

Ans. He ordered his chief engineer. Hamân to build a tall building so he could reach Musâ's (A.S.) God.

Q.63 What are Allâh's signs which Prophet Mûsâ (A.S.) used to convince the Pharaoh?

Ans. A rod which became a serpent and his hand would radiate white.

Q.64 How did the Pharaoh respond to Prophet Musa's (A.S.) signs?

Ans. He called every skilled magician in Egypt to challenge Prophet Mûsâ (A.S.).

Q.65 What happened when the magicians saw Prophet Mûsâ (A.S.)?

Ans. They threw down their rods and they appeared as though they ran about. Prophet Mûsâ (A.S.) threw out his row which swallowed up the magicians false acts. The magicians prostrated and said, "We believe in the Lord of the Worlds, the Lord of Mûsâ (A.S.) and Harûn (A.S.)."

Q.66 What did Allâh order Prophet Mûsâ (A.S.) to do after the Pharoah and his people did not believe?

Ans. To leave Egypt with the people of Israel and cross the sea.

Q.67 What did the Pharoah do after Prophet Mûsâ (A.S.) left Egypt?

Ans. He followed them with an army.

Q.68 How did Allâh save Prophet Mûsâ (A.S.) and his people from the Pharoah's army?

Ans. Allâh inspired Prophet Mûsâ (A.S.) to strike the sea with his rod so the sea was divided. The Pharoah's army was drowned.

Q.69 What did the children of Isra'îl ask Prophet Mûsâ (A.S.) when they were in Sinai?

Ans. First, they asked him to make them an idol god to worship. Second they complained to him about the heat of the sun, the shortage of the varieties of food and water.

Q.70 How did Allâh give the children of Isra'îl bounty while they were in Sinai?

Ans. Allâh gave them the shade of clouds and sent them "manna" (a sweet which comes on the leaves of some tree) and "salwa" (quails, a land of bird) and Allâh ordered Mûsâ (A.S.) to strike the rock with his rod, where twelve springs gushed forth for the twelve tribes of Isra'îl.

Q.71 What is the famous event which happened to Prophet Mûsâ (A.S.) with the children of Isra'îl in Sinai?

Ans. Allâh commanded Prophet Mûsâ (A.S.) to leave his people under the guidance of his brother Harûn (A.S.) (Aaron) and retire to the mountain for forty days to receive the laws. On his return he found his people worshipping a statue of a calf despite Harûn's warning. The calf was burned, the children of Israel repented and Allâh forgave them.

Q.72 What was the attitude of the children of Isra'îl towards Allâh after Prophet Mûsâ's (A.S.) death?

Ans. They broke their covenant with Allâh to follow his commands, killed many of their prophets, changed the word of Allâh for worldly gain, persisted on materialism, did not accept the message of Prophets 'Îsa (A.S.) (Jesus) and Muhammad and did not give gratitude to Allâh who gave them his bounty.

Q.73 How did Allâh punish the children of Isra'îl after Prophet Mûsâ (A.S.) died?

Ans. He declared that he would send against them, until the Day of Judgement, those who would treat them with penalties and that the would break them into sections throughout the world.

Q.74 Where did the children of Isra'îl live after Prophet Musâ's (A.S.) death?

Ans. They lived in Palestine.

Q.75 What was the condition of the children of Isra'îl in Palestine?

Ans. They were not a strong and united nation. They suffered from many conquests from neighbouring nations. Allâh had appointed Taloot (Saul) as King over them, but they raised many objections. Taloot formed an army to fight their enemies lead by Jaloot (Galiath). Prophet Dawûd (A.S.) (David) was in the army of Taloot and he killed Jaloot.

Q.76 What were the favours Allâh bestowed on Dawûd (A.S.)?

Ans. Wisdom, Kingdom, and Prophethood.

Q.77 Who followed Prophet Dawûd (A.S.) in his Kingdom?

Ans. His son Prophet Solaiman (A.S.) (Soloman).

Q.78 What were the favours Allâh bestowed on Prophet Solaimân (A.S.)?

Ans. Allâh had taught him the significance of the bird's voices, made the wind subservient to him, sent clouds with rain in arid areas and many other miracles mentioned in the Holy Qur'ân.

Q.79 Who is the mother of Prophet 'Îsa (A.S.) (Jesus)?

Ans. Maryam (Mary).

Q.80 How was Maryam born and raised?

Ans. Maryam's mother, Imran's wife was expecting to have a male child and she had the intention of dedicating the child to Allâh's service. When she got Maryam, she dedicated her to Allâh's service and she grew up in purity and piety.

Q.81 What did the Angels say to Maryam, before Prophet 'Îsa's (A.S.) birth?

Ans. That Allâh had chosen her and purified her and chosen her above the women of all nations and that she would bear a child, his name would be the Mesiah 'Îsâ (A.S.), son of Maryam and that he would be held in honour in this world and in the Hereafter and should speak to the people in childhood and in maturity.

Q.82 **What was Maryam's reaction to the Angels?**

Ans. She wondered how she could bear a child when she was not married. But she was told that Allâh creates what he wills.

Q.83 **What was the reaction of the people after Prophet Îsâ's (A.S.) birth?**

Ans. They said, "O Maryam, truly you have brought an amazing thing. Your father was not a man of evil, nor was your mother an unchaste woman."

Q.84 **How did Maryam react to her people after they questioned her about Prophet Îsâ's (A.S.) birth?**

Ans. Allâh inspired her to decline all conversation and point to the child who with Allâh's power spoke, "I am indeed a servant of Allâh. He has given me a Revelation and made me a Prophet. And He has made me blessed wheresoever I be, and has enjoined on me prayer and charity as long as I live. He has made me kind to my mother and not overbearing or miserable. So peace be on me the day I was born, the day that I die, and the day that I shall be raised again in the Day of Resurrection."

Q.85 **What did Prophet Îsâ (A.S.) teach the children of Israel?**

Ans. He taught them the Oneness of Allâh the taught them Al-Injîl (Gospel), Allâh's word to guide them.

Q.86 **Is the current Gospel the same as the one Allâh revealed to Prophet Îsâ (A.S.)?**

Ans. No. The true Gospel was lost early in the Christian era when the Christians were weak and when they were persecuted by their enemies. The current Gospel is man written by some disciples and followers of the Prophet Îsâ, some of whom never met Prophet Îsâ (A.S.) himself.

Q.87 **What are some of the miracles given to Prophet Îsâ (A.S.) by Allâh?**

Ans. Reviving the dead, healing the blind and the leprous, telling the people what they ate and store in their homes and making a creation out of clay in the likeness of a bird and breathing into it to become a soaring being, all by the power of Allâh.

Q.88 How did the children of Isrâ'îl react to Prophet Îsâ (A.S.)?

Ans. They conspired against him because they did not like his condemnation of their materialism. They plotted to kill him.

Q.89 Was Prophet Îsâ (A.S.) crucified and killed?

Ans. No. Allâh saved him and raised him up to his Kingdom. Someone in the likeness of Prophet Îsâ (A.S.) was crucified.

Q.90 What are some of the verses of the Qur'ân about the nature of Prophet Îsâ (A.S.)?

Ans. "Surely the case of Jesus with Allâh is like the case of Adam (A.S.). He created him out of the dust, then He said to him "be" and he was", 3:60. "Verily, the Messiah, Jesus, son of Mary, was only a messenger of Allâh and a fulfillment of His word which He sent down to Mary, and a mercy from Him. So believe in Allâh and His messengers and say not "They are three". Desist, it will be better for you. Verify, Allâh is the only one God. Far it is from His holiness that He should have a son.", 4:172.

Q.91 What stories besides Prophet's stories are mentioned in the Qur'ân?

Ans. The story of the companions of the cave (Sûrah 18), the story of Zul-qarnain (Sûrah 18), the story of Luqmân (Sûrah 31) and others.

Q.92 Do Muslims believe in all Prophets mentioned in the Qur'ân?

Ans. Yes, all are Prophets of Allâh, calling to the same and one religion: Islâm (submission to the will and laws of Allâh), Prophet Muhammad (ﷺ) is the last Prophet to all the nations.

Q.93 Were there other Prophets besides the ones mentioned by name in the Qur'ân?

Ans. Allâh tells us in the Qur'ân that there are others besides the ones mentioned by name.

Q.94 Why did Allâh tell us the stories in the Qur'ân?

Ans. The answer is in 12:111, "There is, in their stories, lessons to learn from, for those who understand."

Q.95 Which ayat contains references to the story of Prophet Adam (A.S.)?

Ans. 2:30-39, 7:11-25, 15:26-44, 17:61-65, 18:50, 20:115-126, 38:71-88.

Q.96 Which ayat contains references to the story of Prophet Nûh (A.S.)?

Ans. 7:59-64, 10:71-73, 11:25-49, 21:76-77, 23:23-30, 26:105-122, 29:14-15, 37:75-82, 54:9-17, all of 71.

Q.97 Which ayat contains references to the story of Prophet Hûd (A.S.)?

Ans. 7:65-72, 11:50-60, 23:31-41, 26:123-140, 41:15-16, 46:21-25, 51:41-45, 53:50-55, 54: 18-22, 89:6-14.

Q.98 Which ayat contains references to the story of Prophet Ibrahim (A.S.)?

Ans. 29:16-27, 19:41-48, 6:75-83, 21:51-70, 26:69-83, 37:83-98, 2:258, 37:99-113, 51:24-30, 14:35-41, 2:124-129, 3:96-97, 22:26-27, 2:130-141, 3:67, 6:161-163.

Q.99 Which ayat contains references to the story of Prophet Lût (A.S.)?

Ans. 7:80-84, 11:69-83, 15:51-77, 26:160-175, 27:54-58, 29:28-35, 37:133-138, 51:31-37, 54:33-40.

Q.100 Which ayat contains references to the story of Prophet Shu'aib (A.S.)?

Ans. 7:85-93, 11:85-95, 15:78-79, 26:176-191.

Q.101 Which Âyat contains reference to the story of Prophet Ismâ'îl (A.S.)?

Ans. 37:101-102, 19:54-55, 38:45-48, 21:85-86, 4:163, 2:140.

Q.102 Which ayat contains reference to the story of Prophet Ishaq (A.S.)?

Ans. 37:112-113, 3:84.

Q.103 Which ayat contains references to the story of Prophet Yusuf (A.S.)?

Ans. 12: all.

Q.104 Which ayat contains references to the story of Prophet Aiyûb (A.S.)?

Ans. 21:83-84, 38:41-44.

Q.105 Which ayat contains references to the story of Prophet Zul-Kafil (A.S.)?

Ans. 21:85-86, 38:45-48.

Q.106 Which ayat contains references to the story of Prophet Yunus (A.S.)?

Ans. 10:98, 21:87-88, 37:139-148, 68:48-50.

Q.107 Which ayat contain reference to the story of Prophet Mûsâ (A.S.)?

Ans. 19:51-53, 28:1-32, 20:40-76, 7:127-133, 26:10-19, 23-28, 29-33, 52-68, 7:103-126, 10:75-82, 26:29-51, 40:28-29, 7:130-133, 43:49-56, 44:17-33, 7:136-141, 5:20-26, 2:40-41, 49-57, 60-73, 7:142-148, 20:83-98, 7:155-157, 18:60-82, 28:67-83.

Q.108 Which ayat contains reference to the story of Prophet Ilias (A.S.)?

Ans. 37:123-132.

Q.109 Which ayat contains references to the story of Prophet Dawûd (A.S.)?

Ans. 2:246-251, 34:10-13, 21:79-80, 38:17-20, 4:163, 17:55, 38:21-26.

Q.110 Which ayat contain references to the story of Prophet Solaimân (A.S.)?

Ans. 27:76, 17-44, 38:30-40, 21:78-82, 34:12-14.

Q.111 Which ayat contain references to the story of Prophets Zakaria (A.S.) and Yahya (A.S.)?

Ans. 19:1-15, 3:17-39, 21:89-90.

Q.112 Which ayat contain references to the story of Prophet 'Îsâ (A.S.)?

Ans. 3:33-37, 42-55, 58-93, 19:16-37, 21:89-91, 4:156, 19:88-95, 6:100-103, 4:171-173, 2:87, 116-117, 253, 9:30, 37:149-160, 18:1-5, 10.68-70, 5:17, 72-75, 110-115, 116-118, 39:4-5, 43:81-82, 17:111, 112: all, 10:69-70, 86:17, 61:6-14.

CHAPTER

7

ISLAMIC HISTORY

Q. 1 What does the word Khalifa (Caliph) mean?

Ans. Rule of the Islamic nation.

Q.2 Why are the four Caliphs who were in charge of the Islamic nation after the Prophet called "The Righteous Caliphs"?

Ans. Because of their service to Islam.

Q.3 Who are the Righteous Caliphs?

Ans. Abu Bakr (R.Z.A.), Umar (R.Z.A.), Uthmân (R.Z.A.) and Ali (R.Z.A.). All were companions of Prophet Muhammad (ﷺ).

Q.4 How were the Righteous Caliphs chosen to rule Islamic nation?

Ans. By nominations, then an election by the majority of Muslims.

Q.5 How long did Abu Bakr (R.Z.A.) rule the Muslims?

Ans. Two years and three months.

Q.6 What are the important accomplishments of Abu Bakr (R.Z.A.) as a ruler of the Islamic nation?

Ans. He put down rebelion of some tribes of Arabic and sent an army under Khalid ibn-Al-Walîd (R.Z.A.) to Iraq and an army to Syria under Amr Ibn-Al'as (R.Z.A.) to liberate Iraq and Syria from the Romans and from worshipping other than God, Lord of all Lords.

Q.7 What are the important accomplishment of Umar (R.Z.A.) as ruler of the Islamic nation?

Ans. He sent armies to liberate Persia, Jerusalem, Egypt and Libya.

Q.8 What was the size of the Islamic nation at the time of Umar (R.Z.A.).

Ans. It extended from Arabia in the south to the Carcosus

mountains in the north and the boarders of China in the east and to Libya in the west.

Q.9 Who ruled the Islamic nation after Umar (R.Z.A.)?

Ans. Uthman (R.Z.A.).

Q.10 What are the important accomplishments of Uthman (R.Z.A.) as ruler of the Islamic nation?

Ans. The rest of North Africa was liberated and came under Islamic rule; Tunisia, Algeria and Morocco.

Q.11 Who ruled the Islamic nation after Uthman (R.Z.A.)?

Ans. Ali ibn-Abi-Talib (R.Z.A.).

Q.12 What was the capital of the Islamic nation during the rule of Abu Bakr (R.Z.A.), Umar (R.Z.A.) and Uthman (R.Z.A.)?

Ans. Al-Medina in Arabia.

Q.13 What was the capital of the Islamic nation during the rule of Ali (R.Z.A.)?

Ans. Al-Kûfa in Iraq.

Q.14 What was the year when the era of the four Righteous Caliphs ended?

Ans. 40 A.H.

Q.15 What was the major change in choosing the Muslim ruler after 'Ali (R.Z.A.)?

Ans. The Caliphate became a hereditary system which was incompatible with Islamic teachings which demanded that the Caliph be elected by the consent of the majority of Muslims.

Q.16 Who was the Caliph after 'Ali (R.Z.A.)?

Ans. Mu'awiya ibn Abi-Sufyân (R.Z.A.), the first in Umayya (R.Z.A.) Caliphat.

Q.17 What was the capital of the Islamic nation during the Umayyad (R.Z.A.) Caliphate?

Ans. Damascus in Syria.

Q.18 Why was the period of Caliph Mu'awiya rule and that of his family called "Umayyads" (R.Z.A.)?

Ans. Because he was from an Arabian tribe called "Bani-Umayya".

Q.19 What was the important accomplishment of Mu'awiya (R.Z.A.) as a ruler of the Islamic nation?

Ans. He liberated Turkistan in the north and Sudan in the South.

Q.20 How many years did Caliph Mu'awiya (R.Z.A.) rule?

Ans. Twenty years, he died in 60 A.H.

Q.21 Who succeeded Caliph Mu'awiya (R.Z.A.)?

Ans. His son, then by his grandson, and after by some other Umayyads (R.Z.A.); 14 in succession.

Q.22 How many years did the Umayyad (R.Z.A.) Caliphate last?

Ans. 92 years from 40 A.H. to 132 A.H. (661-750 A.D.).

Q.23 What succeeded the Umayyad (R.Z.A.) Caliphate?

Ans. The Abbaside Caliphate.

Q.24 Why are the Abbaside Caliphates called that?

Ans. Because they are descendant from Al-Abbas; the Prophet's uncle.

Q.25 What was the capital of the Islamic nation during the Abbaside Caliphate?

Ans. Baghdad in Iraq.

Q.26 How many in succession were the Abbaside Caliphate?

Ans. Thirty-seven.

Q.27 Who is the most famous Abbaside Caliph?

Ans. Harûn al-Rashîd and his son Al-Ma'mûn.

Q.28 What ended the Abbaside Caliphate?

Ans. The destruction of Baghdad by the Mongols.

Q.29 How was Baghdad during Caliph Al-Ma'mûn?

Ans. It was a centre of Islamic scholarship (833 A.D.); books were translated from Syriac, Hebrew and Greek. Islamic books were written on every subject and were translated into Latin. This was one of the most important factors which led to the Renaissance in Europe.

Q.30 When did the Abbaside Caliphate end?

Ans. About 651 A.H. (1258 A.D.).

Q.31 Who destroyed Baghdad at the end of the Abbaside Caliphate?

Ans. The Mongols.

Q.32 Who led the Islamic army to liberate Al-Anndalus (Spain)?

Ans. Tariq ibn-Ziyâd (R.Z.A.) and Mûsâ ibn-Nusayr (R.Z.A.).

Q.33 When did the Islamization of Spain occur?

Ans. 95 A.H. (714 A.D.) during the sixth Umayyad Caliph Al-Walid ibn-Abdul-Mâlik (R.Z.A.).

Q.34 What was the capital of Spain during the Islamic rule?

Ans. Granada (Qurtuba).

Q.35 When did the Islamic Rule of Spain end?

Ans. 897 A.H. (1492 A.D.).

Q.36 Did the Muslims in Spain acknowledge the Abbaside Caliphate when it was established in Baghdad?

Ans. No, an Umayyad Caliphate was established there.

Q.37 During the Abbaside Caliphate, Islamic dynasties were established. Name three in Africa and three in Asia.

Ans. In Africa; the Aghlabid Dynasty in Qayrawân, Tunisia (184-296 A.H.), the Fatimid Dynasty in Cairo, Egypt (297-560 A.H.) and the Ayyubide Dynasty in Cairo. Egypt (560-640 A.H.). In Asia; The Samanide Dynasty (261-395 A.H.) and the Gaznawide Dynasty (395-555 A.H.) in central Asia and the Buwayhide Dynasty (333-446 A.H.) in Iran.

Q.38 Who were the Crusaders?

Ans. The Pope of Rome ordered a holy war on the Muslims to deliver Jerusalem from Muslim hands. Many European countries united and made an alliance and the army was referred to as the Crusaders.

Q.39 Who led the Islamic army to victory against the Crusaders?

Ans. Salah-al-Dîn Al-Ayyûby, the first ruler in the Ayyûbide Dynasty in Egypt.

Q.40 Who stopped the advance of the Mongols after the destruction of Baghdad?

Ans. Sultan Bibars of Egypt.

Q.41 What did Sultan Bibars of Egypt do after he defeated the Mongols?

Ans. He established an Abbaside Caliphate in Egypt in name only (660-923 A.H.).

Q.42 Who established the Islamic Caliphate after the Abbaside Caliphate in Egypt?

Ans. The Ottomans in Turkey (1600-1922 A.D.).

Q.43 What are the basic Islamic principles related to governing?

Ans. The ruler is elected by the consent of the majority of Muslims and remains in the office only if he abides by the Islamic teachings and by the "shura" principle (the consultation of the ruled).

Q.44 How many Muslims are in the world today (1987)?

Ans. Over one billion.

Q.45 Which Muslim country are the cities of Macca and Madina in?

Ans. Saudi Arabia.

Q.46 What is the population of Saudi Arabia?

Ans. Seven million.

Q.47 What is the capital of Saudi Arabia?

Ans. Riyadh

Q.48 What is the main characteristic of the land in Saudi Arabia?

Ans. Mostly desert, no rivers, some rain, and dates are the main crop.

Q.49 What are the most important animals in Saudi Arabia?

Ans. The camel and the Arabian horse.

Q.50 What are the national products in Saudi Arabia?

Ans. Oil; Saudi Arabia is the largest oil producing country in the world.

Q.51 What sea separates Saudi Arabia and Egypt?

Ans. The Red Sea.

Q.52 Which Muslim country is the oldest country in the world?
Ans. Egypt, it has a 5,000 year history, it has the pyramids and the sphinx.

Q.53 What is the capital of Egypt?
Ans. Cairo.

Q.54 What is the population of Egypt?
Ans. 60 Million.

Q.55 Who is the Prophet who was raised and preached in Egypt?
Ans. Mûsâ (A.S.).

Q.56 What are the main national products of Egypt?
Ans. Oil, the income from the Suez Canal, and tourism.

Q.57 What are the highlights of things to see in Egypt?
Ans. The river Nile, the longest river in the world. The ancient, the Coptic and Islamic buildings and monuments. The oldest University in the world (over 1000 years old); Al-Azhar where many students from the Islamic world come to study.

Q.58 Which Islamic country was declared Israel in 1948?
Ans. Palestine.

Q.59 What is the Islamic holy place in Palestine?
Ans. Jerusalem where the Aqsa Mosque is located, the third Mosque which a Muslim should visit after visiting the Mosques in Mecca and Madina.

Q.60 Which Prophets lived in Palestine?
Ans. Ibrahim (A.S.), Lût (A.S.), Ismâ'îl (A.S.), Ya'qûb (A.S.), Ishâq (A.S.), Dawûd (A.S.), Solaimân (A.S.), and Îsâ (A.S.).

Q.61 Did Prophet Muhammad (ﷺ) visit Jerusalem?
Ans. Yes, during "Al-Isra and Al-Mi'rag" when he was taken from Macca to Jerusalem and then to the Heavens and returned back to Macca.

Q.62 What is the problem of the Palestinian people, Muslims and Christians?
Ans. The Jews, who lived all over the world started to go to Palestine to live in the 1920's and 1930's. When they became powerful, they took Palestinian's land and homes. They killed

many Palestinians and many more had to run away because they were terrorized. Many today live abroad and many others live in tents and shacks in refugee camps.

Q.63 What are the imortant cities of Palestine?
Ans. Jerusalem, Heifa and Yafa.

Q.64 What are the natural highlights of Palestine?
Ans. The Dead Sea, where there is so much salt that no fish can live in it and you can easily float.

Q.65 What is the Muslim country which is in Europe and Asia?
Ans. Turkey.

Q.66 What is the population of Turkey?
Ans. 50 Million.

Q.67 What are some of the neighbours of Turkey?
Ans. The Soviet Union, Iran, Iraq and Syria.

Q.68 What is the capital of Turkey?
Ans. Ankara.

Q.69 What is the biggest city of Turkey?
Ans. Istanbul. It is a very old city. The Greeks built it 2500 years ago. The Roman Emperor Constantine made it the capital of his Empire in 330 A.D. and called it Constantinople. Sultan Muhammad the second liberated the city in 1453. It remained the capital of Turkey until 1923.

Q.70 What significent event in Turkey's history related to the Muslim nation?
Ans. The established of a wide Islamic state called "The Ottoman State" and this was the most powerful state in the world for 500 years. The head of the state was the Muslim Caliph.

Q.71 What hapened to the "Ottoman State"?
Ans. It got weaker and its enemy, England, France and Russia defeated it.

Q.72 What is the Muslim country which is made up of more than 10,000 islands?
Ans. Indonesia.

Q.73 What is the meaning of Indonesia?
Ans. Indos means East India and Nesos means island.

Q.74 What is the population of Indonesia?
Ans. 135 million, the most populous Islamic country.

Q.75 What language do the Muslims of Indonesia speak?
Ans. Malay.

Q.76 What natural phenomena is present in Indonesia?
Ans. Vulcanoes.

Q.77 What is the capital of Indonesia?
Ans. Jakarta.

Q.78 What is the most populous island in Indonesia?
Ans. Java.

Q.79 What foreign power has occupied Indonesia for 300 years?
Ans. The Dutch.

Q.80 What Muslim country was formed in 1947 in the Indian Subcontinent?
Ans. Pakistan.

Q.81 What are some of the neighbours of Pakistan?
Ans. The Soviet Union, Iran, China, India and Afghanistan.

Q.82 What is the population of Pakistan?
Ans. 90 Million.

Q.83 What is the capital of Pakistan?
Ans. Islamabad.

Q.84 What is the language used in Pakistan?
Ans. Urdu, English and other languages like Sindhi, Punjabi and Pushto.

Q.85 What are the largest cities in Pakistan?
Ans. Karachi and Lahore.

Q.86 What is the Muslim country which is the largest country in Africa?
Ans. Sudan.

Q.87 What is the population of Sudan?
Ans. 20 Million.

Q.88 What language is spoken in Sudan?
Ans. Arabic.

Q.89 What is the capital of Sudan?
Ans. Al'Khartum, meaning in Arabic the trunk of the elephant.

Q.90 What are the main exports of Sudan?
Ans. Arabic Gum (it supplied 80% of the world's consumption of Arabic Gum), cotton, sesame, peanuts, sugar, coffee, dates, and wheat.

Q.91 What is the size of the land which can be cultivated in Sudan?
Ans. 200 million acres.

Q.92 When did Sudan become independent from Britain?
Ans. 1956.

Q.93 What is the Islamic country which used to be called Persia?
Ans. Iran.

Q.94 What is the capital of Iran?
Ans. Tehran.

Q.95 What is the population of Iran?
Ans. 45 million.

Q.96 What is the language used in Iran?
Ans. Persian with Arabic script.

Q.97 What are the natural resources of Iran?
Ans. Oil, minerals, turquoise, grains, pistachio and caviar.

Q.98 What separates Iran and Arabia?
Ans. The Persian Gulf.

Q.99 What is the most famous export from Iran?
Ans. Oil and rugs.

Q.100 What is the famous Iranian city for Islamic education and for its University?
Ans. Qum.

Q.101 What is the important event which happened in Iran in 1979?

Ans. The Muslim scholars of Iran and the people of Iran revolted against the Shah and established the Islamic Republic of Iran.

Q.102 What European country has more than 70% Muslims?

Ans. Albania.

Q.103 Which countries have large Muslim minority populations (30 million or more)?

Ans. China (70 million), India (100 million) and the Soviet Union (30 million).

Q.104 What are the Muslim countries in Asia (Muslim population over 70%)?

Ans. Afghanistan, Bahruin, Bangladesh, Brunei, Indonesia, Iran, Iraq, Jammu and Kashmir, Jordan, Kuwait, Lebanon, Malaysia, Maldives, Oman, Pakistan, Palestine, Qatar, Saudi Arabia, South Yemen, Syria, Turkey, United Arab Emirates, Yemen Arab Republic.

Q.105 What is the total Muslim population in Asia?

Ans. 600 million.

Q.106 What are the Muslim countries in Africa (Muslim population over 70%)?

Ans. Algeria, Benin (Dahomey), Cameron, Central African Republic, Chad, Egypt, Gabon, Gambia, Guinea, Guinea-Bissou, Ethiopia, Ivory Coast, Libya, Malawi, Mali, Djibouti, Mauritania, Niger, Nigeria, Reunion Island, Senegal, Sierra Leone, Somalia, Sudan, Tanzania, Togo, Tunisia, and Upper Volta.

Q.107 What is the total Muslim population in Africa?

Ans. 300 million.

Q.108 What is the total Muslim population in Europe?

Ans. 60 million.

Q.109 What is the total Muslim population in Canada and the U.S.?

Ans. 6 million.

Q.110 What is the total Muslim population in South America?

Ans. 1 million.

Q.111 What is the total Muslim population in Australia and New Zealand?
Ans. 200,000

Q.112 What is the total Muslim population in the world?
Ans. About 1 billion: over 25% of the world's population.

Q.113 Which part of the Soviet Union do the Muslims live?
Ans. The south-eastern part in the Soviet Republics of Turkmenistan, Tajikistan, Kirghizistan, Bashkiristan and Tataristan.

Q.114 Who is the great Islamic Scholars who come from Bashkiristan?
Ans. Imam Al-Bukhâri.

Q.115 What did the communists promise the Muslims when they took power in 1917 in the Soviet Union?
Ans. Protection and religious freedom.

Q.116 Did the communists keep their promises?
Ans. No, they closed Islamic schools and Mosques, forced Muslims to use the Latin alphabet instead of the Arabic one, arrested most of the Imams and sent them into exile in Siberia because their constitution does not believe in Religion, "The teaching of any religious faith whatsoever is not allowed in state, social or private educational institutions.".

Q.117 When did the first Muslims come to Canada?
Ans. The 1871 Canadian census shows that there were 13 Muslims that year, in a population of 3.5 million.

Q.118 What are the different backgrounds of the Muslims in Canada?
Ans. About 40% are from Arabic backgrounds, 40% are from Indian and Pakistani backgrounds and the rest are from other backgrounds.

Q.119 What is the composition of Muslims in Canada regarding their jobs?
Ans. 35% professionals (engineers, doctors,...etc.)
20% skilled workers
20% white collar workers

10% business people
15% others

Q.120 When and where was the first Mosque built in Canada?
Ans. In 1938 in Edmonton, Alberta.

Q.121 Where is the largest population of Muslims in Canada?
Ans. In Ontario.

Q.122 In what year was the League of Arab States founded?
Ans. 1945.

Q.123 In what year was the Islamic Conference of Muslim states first held?
Ans. 1981.

Q.124 In which city was the Bayt al Hikmat (House of Learning) founded by Harûn Al-Rashîd in 830 A.D. which was the key to the development of today's science?
Ans. Baghdad.

Q.125 Mention some of the famous early Muslim astronomers.
Ans. Al-Khawarzmi (also the famous Mathematician who developed the algorithms named after him), Al-Biruni, Al-Farghani (named in the west Alfraganus), Al-Battani, Al-Haytham (Alhazemi), Al-Zarqali (Azarquiel) and Al-Bitruji (Alpertrangius).

Q.126 Mention some of the famous early Muslim scientists who explained the philosophy of nature based upon the atomistic viewpoint governed by the Laws of its Creator.
Ans. Ibn Rushd (Averroes), Al-Ghazzali, Al-Nazzam.

Q.127 What inspires Muslim scientists to seek knowledge and explore?
Ans. The Qur'ân.

Q.128 Mention some of the famous early Muslim Mathematicians.
Ans. Al-Khwarzmi, Al-Uqlidusi, Jabir Ibn Hayyan, Al-Hasib, Al-Battani, Ibn Yunus.

Q.129 Mention some of the famous early Muslims who worked in the field of Geography.
Ans. Al-Kwarzami, Al-Maqdisi, Ibn Batuta, Al-Hamadani, Al-Hamawi, Al-Masudi.

Q.130 Mention some of the famous early Muslim scientists who worked in the area of mineralogy.

Ans. Al-Kindi, Al-Jahiz, Al-Razi, Ibn Sina (Avicenna), Al-Biruni, Al-Tusi, Al-Qazani (Kashani).

Q.131 Mention some of the famous early Muslim scientists who worked in the area of botany.

Ans. Jabir Ibn Hayyan, Al-Ansari, Al-Razi, Ibn Ishaq, Ibn Rushd.

Q.132 Mention some of the famous early Muslim Scientists who worked in the area of zoology.

Ans. Ibn Shumayle, Ibn Al-Arabi, Al-Farabi, Al-Kindi, Ibn Sina, Ibn Rushd.

Q.133 Mention some of the famous early Muslim Physicians and Surgeons.

Ans. Ibn Sina, Al-Zahrawi, Ibn Nafis, Ibn Al-Quff. Ibn Sina wrote his reference book in medicine, which was used in Europe for 500 years.

Q.134 Mention some of the famous early Muslim ophthalmologists.

Ans. Abu Ruh Muhammad Al-Jurani, Hunayn Ibn Ishaq, Ali Ibn Isa.

Q.135 Mention some of the famous early Muslim scientists who worked in the field of chemistry.

Ans. Jabir Ibn Hayyan, Al-Razi, Al-Farabi, Ibn Sina, Al-Kathi.

Q.136 Mention some of the famous early Muslim scientists who worked in the area of physiology.

Ans. Al-Ghazzali, Ibn Arabi, Al-Baydawi, Ibn Al-Nafis.

Q.137 Mention some of the scientific subjects whose basics have been treated in the Qur'ân and the Sunnah.

Ans. Astronomy, physics, history, anthropology, geography, natural history, biology, origin of life, botany, zoology, economy, sociology, psychology, sexology and medicines.

Q.138 Mention three famous Muslim women who set excellent models for women over the world.

Ans. Khadeeja (R.Z.A.) (first wife of the Prophet)

Fatima (R.Z.A.) (the youngest of the four daughters of the Prophet (ﷺ))

A'isha (R.Z.A.) (the Prophet's (ﷺ) wife after the death of his first wife).

Q.139 How did Khadeejah (R.Z.A.) contribute to Islam?

Ans. She was the first Muslim, stood by the Prophet (ﷺ) giving him encouragement and comfort. She suffered greatly by the side of her husband through difficult times: the deaths of their sons Qasim and Abdullah in their infancy, the migration of their daughter Ruqaiyyah with her husband Uthman Ibn Affan (R.Z.A.) to Abyssinia and the boycott of the Prophet's (ﷺ) family for three years.

Q.140 True or False: Khadeejah (R.Z.A.) is the mother of all the Prophet's children except Ibrahim.

Ans. True.

Q.141 What was the job of Khadeejah (R.Z.A.) before marrying the Prophet (ﷺ)?

Ans. She was a business woman of wealth and highly regarded by her country's people.

Q.142 True or False: Khadeejah (R.Z.A.) was married twice before marrying the Prophet (ﷺ).

Ans. True.

Q.143 When did Khadeejah (R.Z.A.) die?

Ans. 3 years before Hijra.

Q.144 What are the names of the daughters of Khadeejah (R.Z.A.) and the Prophet (ﷺ)?

Ans. Zainab (R.Z.A.), Ruqayya (R.Z.A.), Umm Kulthum (R.Z.A.) and Fatimah (R.Z.A.).

Q.145 How did Fatimah (R.Z.A.) contribute to Islam?

Ans. Fatimah (R.Z.A.) served her father with love and devotion and her husband Ali with same. She kept close to her father and followed his example, participated in all the hardships the Muslims faced.

Q.146 How many children did Fatimah (R.Z.A.) and Ali (R.Z.A.) have?

Ans. Five, three sons, Hasan (R.Z.A.), Husain (R.Z.A.), and

Muhassin (R.Z.A.) who died while a baby and two daughters Zainab (R.Z.A.) and Umm Kul<u>th</u>um (R.Z.A.).

Q.147 When did Fatimah (R.Z.A.) die?

Ans. A few months after the Prophet (ﷺ) on the 3rd of Ramadan in 11 A.H. at the age of 30.

Q.148 When was A'isha (R.Z.A.) married to the Prophet (ﷺ)?

Ans. She married him after the death of his first wife Khadeejah. (R.Z.A.) The marriage contract was performed when she was 9 and she lived with him when she was 12 or 15.

Q.149 Who was 'Aisha's (R.Z.A.) father?

Ans. Abu Bakr (R.Z.A.), the closest friend and companion of the Prophet (ﷺ) and the first Khalifah of Islam.

Q.150 How did 'Aisha (R.Z.A.) contribute to Islam?

Ans. She was a great lady, excellent wife with a wonderful memory, intelligent, had a great love for learning and a sharp sense of judgement.

Q.151 How was 'Aisha (R.Z.A.) involved in the Hijrah to Madina?

Ans. She and her sister Asma' (R.Z.A.) helped the Prophet (ﷺ) and their father pack for the trip.

Q.152 How did 'Aisha (R.Z.A.) work in her house?

Ans. She used to do the household work including grinding flour, baking bread, and making water ready for cooking and drinking.

Q.153 Was 'Aisha (R.Z.A.) around when the Prophet (ﷺ) died?

Ans. Yes, in 11 A.H., the Prophet (ﷺ) fell ill and 'Aisha (R.Z.A.) nursed him with all the love and care of a devoted wife. He died in her lap.

Q.154 How many Hadîth did 'Aisha (R.Z.A.) narrate?

Ans. Over 2,000.

Q.155 When did 'Aisha (R.Z.A.) die?

Ans. On Ramadan 17, 58 A.H., at the age of 67.

CHAPTER 8

LEGAL RULINGS AND THE LAWFUL AND PROHIBITED (AL-HALAL AND AL-HARAM)

Q. 1 What is the basic Islamic principle regarding diet?

Ans. All the things which are pure in themselves and good are lawful as long as they are taken in moderate quantities and all the things which are impure and harmful are unlawful under all ordinary circumstances.

Q.2 What are the foods and drinks which are Haram (Islamically unlawful)?

Ans. Meat of dead animals and birds, flesh of swine, anything slaughtered in any name other than Allâh and all intoxicant drugs and drinks.

Q.3 What are the clothing and adornment which are forbidden for Muslim men?

Ans. Silk material and gold.

Q.4 What is the basic teaching for Muslim men and women when they see or talk to the other sex?

Ans. To lower their gaze and guard their modesty.

Q.5 Does Islam encourage sports and amusements?

Ans. Anything that provokes sound thinking or refreshes the mind and revitalizes the body to keep people healthy is encouraged as long as it does not involve any sin or cause any harm or delay or hamper the fulfillment of other obligations.

Q.6 What are Mazhab (Islamic School of Scholarship and jurists)?

Ans. The four main ones are Maliki, Hanafi, Shafi'i, Hanbali. Among the others are Zaidi and Ja'fari.

Q.7 Is it obligatory that a Muslim follow one of these Mazhab in all its teachings?

Ans. No. The founders of these Islamic Schools are great jurists which contributed to the understanding of Qur'ân and Sunnah and to formalizing Islamic Laws. A Muslim may follow any jurist's opinion on any topic. All Mazhab are the same in the essentials of Islam.

Q.8 Does Islam teach that a woman is to be blamed for Adam's (A.S.) first mistake.

Ans. No.

Q.9 Does Islam teach that Allâh had forgiven both Adam (A.S.) and his wife?

Ans. Yes.

Q.10 Can women reach a high degree in the sight of Allâh by their good deeds?

Ans. Yes.

Q.11 What is Qwa-ma?

Ans. Under normal circumstances, man is responsible for his household and his family and he is the one in charge.

Q.12 True or False: Mistreatment of Muslim women occurs when traditions and selfish ends become more important than Allâh's will and Law.

Ans. True.

Q.13 True or False: In Islam, differences in roles and responsibilities between men and women means complementary roles, not conflicting roles of both sexes in life.

Ans. True.

Q.14 True or False: In Islam, women had political rights for more than 1400 years including election, nomination and participation in public affairs.

Ans. True.

Q.15 True or False: In Islam, women have the following rights: her possessions before marriage do not transfer to spouse, she keeps her maiden name and she has no obligation to spend on her husband and children out of her wealth or income after marriage.

Ans. True.

Q.16 True or False: In Islam, the woman's share of the inheritance is one-half the man's share because men must provide maintenance for wife, children and needy female relatives regardless of wealth of his wife.

Ans. True.

Q.17 True or False: Islam does not forbid women seeking employment if Islamic society can benefit from their exceptional talent or if working becomes necessary and if duties at home, such as raising children are met properly.

Ans. True.

Q.18 True or False: In Islam, the most important role for a woman is as a wife and as a mother.

Ans. True.

Q.19 True or False: Islamic law grants women independent ownership over 1400 years ago. In other societies women were deprived of such law as recently as this 20th century.

Ans. True.

Q.20 True or False: In Islam, kindness to parents is next to worship of Allâh.

Ans. True.

Q.21 True or False: Prophet Muhammad (ﷺ) said: "The most perfect believers are the best in conduct and the best of you are those who are best to their wives.

Ans. True.

Q.22 With whom do family decisions ultimately rest?

Ans. The husband.

Q.23 In marriage, who gives the Mahr (marriage gift) and who receives it?

Ans. The husband gives it as a gift of love and affection to his wife and it belongs to her.

Q.24 Does a woman have to consent before marrying a man?

Ans. Yes.

Q.25 What is Al-Halal?

Ans. That which is permitted and lawful and no restriction exists and the doing of which is allowed by Allâh.

Q.26 What is Al-Haram?

Ans. That which is prohibited by Allâh and unlawful and whoever does it is punished by the law in this life and is punished by Allâh in the Hereafter.

Q.27 What is Al-Makruh?

Ans. That which is less in degree than the haram.

Q.28 Does prohibiting the Halal and permitting the haram similar to committing shirk (setting up partners with Allâh)?

Ans. Yes, because Allâh and Allâh alone is the absolute Law-Giver.

Q.29 Why does Allâh prohibit certain actions?

Ans. Because of their impurity and harmfulness.

Q.30 Does any action which could lead to haram also haram?

Ans. Yes, for example, Islam has prohibited sex outside marriage. It has also prohibited anything which leads to it or makes it attractive, such as seductive clothing, private meetings and casual mixing between men and women, the depiction of nudity, pornographic material, obscene songs, and so on.

Q.31 Do good intentions make haram acceptable?

Ans. No. Islam never supports "the ends justify the means". For example, if one wants to build a mosque or a charitable foundation through a lottery (gambling) then his actions are still haram.

Q.32 What should a Muslim do if he/she is in doubt if something is haram?

Ans. He/she should avoid it.

Q.33 Is "Necessity dictates exceptions" an Islamic principle?

Ans. Yes, for example, only under the compulsion of necessity, a Muslim is permitted to eat a prohibited food in quantities sufficient to save him/her from death if no other food is available.

Q.34 What is haram regarding food?

Ans. Flesh of dead animals (died of a natural death, killing by strangling or by beating or by falling or being gored and that which has been partly eaten by a wild beast), blood, flesh of swine and any animal which has been dedicated to any other than Allâh.

Q.35 Is it haram to use the skin, bones or hair of dead animals?

Ans. No. The prohibition is only concerning eating the dead animal flesh.

Q.36 Are all marine animals (who live in water cannot survive outside it) halal to eat?

Ans. Yes.

Q.37 Is it halal to eat wild animals with a canine tooth (e.g. lion, leopard, wolf..) who prey on others and birds with claws (e.g. hawk, eagle, falcon..)?

Ans. No.

Q.38 What is the Islamic way of slaughtering domesticated animals (cows, poultry, other foul, camels)?

Ans. The animal should be slaughtered by a sharp object which is capable of making it bleed by severing blood vessels and to mention the name of Allâh for giving this bounty.

Q.39 Is it halal for Muslims to eat the flesh of the animals which are lawful, that have been slaughtered or hunted by the people of the book (Jews and Christians)?

Ans. Yes.

Q.40 Are all forms of intoxicants and gambling haram for Muslims?

Ans. Yes.

Q.41 Is it haram to trade in intoxicants or gambling tickets?

Ans. Yes.

Q.42 Should a Muslim stay away from drinking parties?

Ans. Yes.

Q.43 Are drugs such as marijuana, cocaine, and opium haram?

Ans. Yes.

Q.44 What are the two purposes of clothing in Islam?

Ans. To cover the body and to beautify the appearance.

Q.45 What are the two kinds of adornment which are prohibited for men while some are permitted for women?

Ans. Gold and pure silk.

Q.46 What is the dress code for Muslim women?

Ans. It is haram for women to wear clothes which fail to cover the body except the hands and face, transparent or tightly fitted.

Q.47 Is it haram for men to imitate women and for women to imitate men?

Ans. Yes.

Q.48 Is it halal to pride oneself to dress to look superior?

Ans. No.

Q.49 Is it halal to be excessively involved with person beauty like tattooing, undergoing surgery for beautification, plucking the eyebrows, wearing wigs...etc.?

Ans. No.

Q.50 What is the Islamic rule regarding growing a beard for men?

Ans. To let the beard grow and to trim the moustache.

Q.51 Does Islam prohibit keeping statues in the house?

Ans. Yes.

Q.52 Does Islam approve of erecting statues in honour of or in the memory of heroes?

Ans. No.

Q.53 Does Islam approve of children playing with dolls or figures of humans and animals?

Ans. Yes.

Q.54 Does Islam approve figures to be printed on plain surfaces such as paper, cloth, curtains, walls .. etc.?

Ans. There is no general ruling. Each case is judged individually and depends on what the picture depicts, where it is placed and what is its use.

Q.55 What is the Islamic rule regarding photography?

Ans. Most Islamic jurists ruled that photographs are allowed especially for needs such as identity cards, passports and for instructional purposes.

Q.56 Does Islam allow keeping dogs as pets?

Ans. No, mainly because of health hazards.

Q.57 Does Islam allow keeping watch dogs or using them for hunting or guarding cattle or crops?

Ans. Yes.

Q.58 Is smoking tabacco haram?

Ans. Most Islamic jurists ruled that it is haram. Few ruled that it is makruh (highly discouraged). None ruled that is halal.

Q.59 Is any type of trade halal?

Ans. Yes, except those which involve injustice, cheating, making exorbitant profits or the promotion of something which is haram; alcoholic beverages, idols, drugs, etc.

Q.60 Does Islam allow a man and a woman to be in a private sitting (khulwah) without the presence of close relatives (mohrem)?

Ans. No, to guard against sexual temptation.

Q.61 What is the Islamic rule regarding looking at the opposite sex?

Ans. Not to look with desire and to lower their gazes.

Q.62 Is looking at the 'awrah (private parts) of any person (of the same or opposite sex) with or without desire forbidden?

Ans. Yes, it is haram.

Q.63 What is the 'awrah (private parts) of a man?

Ans. It is from the navel to the knees.

Q.64 What is the 'awrah of a woman?

Ans. Her entire body except the face and hands.

Q.65 Why is marriage to more than one woman permitted in Islam?

Ans. For example, in special cases where women outnumber men or the wife cannot bear children, the man is permitted to retain a first wife with all her rights guaranteed and marry a second. Note that in the West (who attack Islam for permitting up to four wifes (restricted polygramy) with the condition of equal and just treatment for all) allows their men to have any number of girlfriends without any legal or moral accountability.

Q.66 Can a woman state in her marriage contract that her husband cannot marry another wife in the future before first divorcing her?

Ans. Yes.

Q.67 Can a husband and his wife have sexual intercourse while she is menstruating?

Ans. No, but other sexual contacts are allowed.

Q.68 Does Islam forbid any postures of sexual intercourse?

Ans. Yes, anal intercourse is forbidden.

Q.69 What is the instruction of Islam regarding the intimate relationship between spouses?

Ans. To regard it as secret and never discuss it in a gathering or speak about it to friends.

Q.70 Is the use of contraception between husband and wife allowed?

Ans. Yes, to plan the family for valid reasons and for recognized necessities.

Q.71 Is abortion allowed?

Ans. After a foetus is completely formed and has been given a soul, abortion is haram.

Q.72 True or False: Divorce is lawful in Islam only when living together becomes very difficult and mutual communications are completely broken and all efforts to save the marriage have failed.

Ans. True.

Q.73 True or False: The woman who cannot bear to live with her husband has the right to obtain divorce by returning to her husband the mahr (marriage gift given to her from her husband).

Ans. True.

Q.74 True or False: It is haram for the husband to mistreat his wife to compel her to seek divorce.

Ans. True.

Q.75 True or False: It is haram for a man or a woman to adopt a son or daughter and treat him/her as a natural son or daughter.

Ans. True.

Q.76 True or False: It is permissible to adopt a child to upbring and educate without being a member of the family (with all the rights of inheritance,..etc).

Ans. True.

Q.77 True or False: Artificial insemination by the husband to his wife is permissible.

Ans. True.

Q.78 Is seeking knowledge mandatory for men and women?

Ans. Yes.

Q.79 Are women allowed to enter the mosque?

Ans. Yes, except during their menses.

Q.80 True or False: It is haram for a father or mother to deprive his or her children of inheritance.

Ans. True.

Q.81 True or False: Disobedience and insulting parents is a major sin.

Ans. True.

Q.82 True or False: Men can volunteer for jihad (Islamic defense) without their parents permission.

Ans. False.

Q.83 True or False: Muslims should be respectful to their non-Muslim parents even if they are arguing with them to renounce Islam.

Ans. True.

Q.84 True or False: It is haram to believe that a person can tell others about their past and future.

Ans. True.

Q.85 True or False: It is not haram if a person hang or carry a charm for good luck.

Ans. False.

Q.86 True or False: Islam forbids any call for nationalism or racism.

Ans. True.

Q.87 True or False: It is halal to be proud of your forefathers and family name and wealth.

Ans. False.

Q.88 Is it allowed in Islam to show excessive grief for the dead and practice wailing?

Ans. No. A Muslim is allowed to show sadness but not to wear mourning clothes or bands or practise wailing.

Q.89 True or False: A wife is not allowed to remarry after the death of her husband.

Ans. False.

Q.90 Is it Islamically allowed to sell and buy goods in free market according to the law of supply and demand?

Ans. Yes, without price manipulation.

Q.91 True or False: It is haram to compel people to sell their goods at a price which is not acceptable to them.

Ans. True.

Q.92 True or False: It is haram to withhold a necessary commodity from the market until it becomes scarce and its price rises.

Ans. True.

Q.93 True or False: It is halal to use a mediator between the buyer and the seller.

Ans. True.

Q.94 True or False: It is halal to increase wealth through trade but it is haram to increase it through lending on usury or interest (riba).

Ans. True.

Q.95 What are some of the reasons of prohibiting interest?

Ans. 1. Dependence on interest prevents people from working to earn money as the lender earns without working.
2. With interest, the rich get richer and the poor get poorer.
3. Taking interest discourages people from helping one another in case of need.
4. Taking interest creates socio-economic classes in the society and leads to social unrest.

Q.96 True or False: It is allowed to make advance payment for a specified price of certain goods.

Ans. True.

Q.97 True or False: It is allowed to have a partnership between capital and labour in business.

Ans. True.

Q.98 True or False: Islam encourages Muslims to enjoy humour, laughter, sport and games as long as it does not involve haram.

Ans. True.

Q.99 What are the sports which are recommended in Islam?

Ans. Anything which require skill and involve physical exercises, for example, racings, wresting, archery, hunting, horseback riding and swimming.

Q.100 True or False: Any game like chess is halal to play as long as no gambling is involved and it does not take time from important duties including performing Salah.

Ans. True.

Q.101 True or False: Singing and music are permitted in Islam as long as they do not involve obscene or propagate unislamic morals.

Ans. True.

Q.102 True or False: Watching movies and plays are permitted in Islam as long as they do not involve obscene or propagate un Islamic morals.

Ans. True.

Q.103 True or False: It is haram for a Muslim to break ties with another, after a quarrel, for more than three days.

Ans. True.

Q.104 True or False: If two Muslims fight each other, the murderer and the murdered will each be in Hell.

Ans. True, because each had the intention of killing the each other.

Q.105 True or False: Islam recommends capital punishment if any of the following crimes are proven to be committed: murder, committing adultery if married and denouncing Islam after willingly accepting it.

Ans. True.

Q.106 True or False: Suicide is a sin.

Ans. True.

Q.107 True or False: It is a religious duty on every Muslim, male and female to seek knowledge, acquire new skills, be physically and mentally strong.

Ans. True.

REFERENCES

CHAPTER - 1

1. A. Von Deuffer. "Ulum Al-Qur'ân", The Islamic Foundation, 1983.
2. K. Murad, "Way to the Qur'ân, The Islamic Foundation, 1985.
3. T.B. Irving, K. Ahmad and M.M. Ahsan, "The Qur'ân, Basic Teachings", 1979.
4. Sayyid Qutb, "In the Shade of the Qur'ân, Vol 30", MWH London Publishers, 1979.
5. T.B. Irving, "The Qur'ân Selections for the Noble Reading", Unity Publishing Company, 1980 and "The Qur'ân, English Translation", Amana Books, 1985.
6. M. Pickthall, "Qur'ânic Advices", Kitab Bhavan, 1984
7. N.J. Dawood, "English Translation - The Koran", Penguin Books, 1968
8. A.J. Arberry, "English Translation - The Koran Interpreted", Oxford University Press. 1983.
9. M.H. Shakir, "English Translation - Holy Qur'ân", Tahrike Tarsill Qur'ân Inc., 1985.
10. M. Pickthall, "English Translation - The Meaning of the Glorious Qur'ân", Taj Company Ltd., India
11. M. Asad, "English Translation - The Message of the Qur'ân", Dar-Al-Andolus, 1980
12. J. Rafai, "English Translation - The Qur'ân; Translation and Study, Juz I", Ta Ha. Publishers, 1984
13. S. Abul A'la Maududi, "English Translation - The Holy Qur'ân", Islamic Publications Ltd., 1982.
14. M.T. Al-Hilali and M.M. Khan. "English Translation - Interpretation of the Meaning of the Noble Qur'ân", The Library of Islam, 1986.
15. A. Yusuf Ali, "English Translation - The Holy Qur'ân", Amana Corp., 1983.

16. M. Ben Nabi, "The Qur'ânic Phenomenon", American Trust Publications, 1983.
17. A. Rahman, "Qur'ânic Sciences", The Muslim Schools Trust, London, 1981
18. M. Bucaille, "The Bible, the Qur'ân and Science". North American Trust Publications. 1979
19. A. Deedat, "What the Bible says about Mhammed", The Islamic Propagation Centre.
20. A.A. Ali, "Science in the Qur'ân", MD Abu Bakr, 1976

CHAPTER — 2

1. M. Azizullah, "Glimpses of the Hadith", The Crescent Publications, 1980.
2. E. Ibrahim and D.J. Davies, "Forty Hadith", The Holy Koran Publishing House, 1978.
3. A. Von Denffer, "Literature on Hadith in European Languages - A Bibliography", The Islamic Foundation, 1981.
4. The Place of Hadith in Islam, The Muslim Students' Association of US and Canada, 1977.
5. A.M. Azami, "Studies in Early Hadith Literature", American Trust Publications, 1978.
6. M.M. Khan, "English Translation and Original, Sahih Al Bukhari", Kitab Bhawan. 1980.
7. A.H. Siddiqi, "English Translation, Sahih Muslim", Kitab Bhawan, 1984.
8. J. Robson, "English Translation, Mishkat Al-Masabih", Sh. M. Ashraf, 1973.
9. F. Karim, "English Translation and Original, Al-Hadith", Mulik Sirajuddin & Sons, 1979.

CHAPTER — 3

1. A. Rahman, "Encyclopaedia of Seerah", Vol 1-4, The Muslim Schools Trust, London, 1981.

2. M.H. Haykal, "The Life of Muhammad", Shorouk Int., 1983
3. L. Azzam and A. Gouverneur, "The Life of the Prophet Muhammad", The Islamic Texts Society, 1985.
4. M.A. Tarantino, "Marvellous Stories from the Life of Muhammad", The Islamic Foundation, 1982.

CHAPTER - 4

1. M. Ali, "The Religion of Islam", The Arab Writer Publishers & Printing.
2. M. Bucaille, "What is the Origin of Man", Publisher Seghers, 1983.
3. M.A. Siddiqui, "Elementary Teachings of Islam", Taj Company Ltd.
4. H. Abdalati, "Islam in Focus". American Trust Publications.
5. S. Islahi. "Islam at a Glance", Markazi Maktaba Islam, 1978.
6. M. Muhammad. "Lessons in Islam", Kifayatullah Sahib.1985.
7. G. Sarwar, "Islam, Beliefs and Teachings", The Muslim Educational Trust, 1982.
8. A.H. Mahmud. "The Creed of Islam", World of Islam Festival Trust, 1978.
9. I.R. al-Faruqi. "Tawhid", Int. Institute of Islamic Thought, 1982.

CHAPTER - 5

1. M.A. Siddiqui, "Elementary Teachings of Islam", Taj Company Ltd.
2. H. Abdalati, "Islam in Focus", American Trust Publications.
3. S. Islahi, "Islam at a Glance", Markazi Maktaba Islami, 1978.
4. M. Muhammad, "Lessons in Islam", Kifayatullah Sahib, 1985.
5. G. Sarwar, "Islam, Beliefs and Teachings", The Muslim Educational Trust, 1982.
6. A. Sabiq, "Fiqh-us-Sunnah-Part 1", American Trust Publications, 1985.
7. Al-Ghazali, "Inner Dimensions of Islamic Worship", The Islamic Foundation, 1983.

8. S. Haneef, "What Eevryone Should Know About Islam and Muslims", Kazi Publications, 1979.

9. A. Rahman, "Prayer, Its Significance and Benefits", The Muslim Schools Trust, London, 1979.

CHAPTER — 6

1. A.M.R. Muhajir, "Lessons from the Stories of the Qur'ân", Sh. M. Ashraf, 1980.

CHAPTER — 7

1. G. Sarwar, "Islam, Beliefs and Teachings", The Muslim Educational Trust, 1982.
2. A.H.A. Nadwi, "Islam and the World", IFSO, 1977.
3. J. Zaydan, "History of Islamic Civilization", Kitab Bhavan, 1981.
4. R. Ahmad and S.N. Admad, "Quest for New Science", Centre for Studies on Science, 1984.
5. M.T. Quraishi, "Islam: A Way of Life and A Movement", American Trust Publications, 1984.
6. A. Rahman, "Qur'ânic Sciences", The Muslim Schools Trust, London, 1981.

CHAPTER — 8

1. Y. Al-Qaradawi, "The Lawful and The Prohibited in Islam", American Trust Publications, 1980.
2. As-Sayyid Sabiq, "Fiqh-Us-Sunnah", American Trust Publications, 1985.